THE CHANGING RIVER

Thames watermen hustling a customer at Wapping,
by Rowlandson, 1812.

THE CHANGING RIVER

Anthony Burton

LONDON
VICTOR GOLLANCZ LTD
1982

British Library Cataloguing in Publication Data
Burton, Anthony
　The changing river.
　1. Rivers—Great Britain
　I. Title
　551.48′3′0941　　　GB1283
　ISBN 0-575-02967-6

The verses from 'Puck's Song' in *The Definitive Edition of Rudyard Kipling's Verse* are quoted by permission of A. P. Watt Ltd.

The lines from *Four Quartets* by T. S. Eliot are quoted by permission of Faber and Faber Ltd.

Photoset in Great Britain by
Rowland Phototypesetting Limited, Bury St Edmunds, Suffolk
and printed by St Edmundsbury Press
Bury St Edmunds, Suffolk

For Pip who did all the hard work

Contents

7

Illustrations

Frontispiece

Thames watermen hustling a customer at Wapping, by
Rowlandson (*Guildhall Library, City of London*)

Following page 30

A medieval mixed fishery (*British Library*)

A medieval float-fisherman (*Piscatorial Society*)

A medieval mining scene (*Science Museum, London*)

An example of the use of water power from a German treatise of
1617 (*Science Museum, London*)

Following page 48

Water mills, drawn by the celebrated water-colourist, David
Cox.

A view of the Thames below Westminster Pier by Wenceslaus
Hollar (*The Barber Institute of Fine Arts, Birmingham University*)

Pleasure boating on Chelsea Reach, by Rowlandson (*Guildhall
Library, City of London*)

A river scene in Norwich in the early nineteenth century (*Bodleian
Library, Oxford – Gough. Adds. Fol. A.104 plt 31*)

Liverpool docks at the beginning of the nineteenth century
(*Bodleian Library, Oxford – G. A. Gen. Top. vol. 2. opp. 81*)

The viaduct across the River Nidd at Knaresborough (*Science
Museum, London*)

9

Punt fishing, mid-nineteenth century (*Piscatorial Society*)

Eel anglers, 1834 (*Piscatorial Society*)

Following page 80

The entrance to the River Fleet (*Guildhall Library, City of London*)

The old London Bridge and the new bridge under construction in 1830 (*Science Museum, London*)

The iron bridge across the River Wear, Sunderland, in 1798 (*Science Museum, London*)

Goole docks in 1905 (*Michael Ware*)

Abbey Cloth Mills at Bradford-on-Avon (*Ironbridge Gorge Museum Trust*)

Fulling stocks at Otterburn Mills (*Ironbridge Gorge Museum Trust*)

Following page 112

Marlow Lock with steam launch in the 1880s (*Oxford City Library*)

Henry Taunt beside Wallingford Bridge (*Oxford City Library*)

Wickerwork fish weirs on the River Severn (*Gloucester City Museums*)

Severn fishermen tarring nets in 1897 (*Gloucester City Museums*)

A Thames barge (*Alexander Cordell*)

A Humber keel (*George E. Byers*)

A train of Tom Puddings taking coal to Goole (*Michael Ware*)

A river steamer on the Severn pulling a convoy of narrow boats (*Michael Ware*)

CHAPTER ONE

Veins in the national body

'River', declares the *Oxford English Dictionary* amidst a selection of alternative definitions, 'the boundary between life and death'. It is not perhaps the version that first comes to mind, unless one is a classicist thinking of the River Styx or a Scots enthusiast for the works of Burns—if indeed there is any other type of Scot—who would remember the lines:

> And hast thou crost that unknown river,
> Life's dreary bound?

An odd definition, then, yet one that has in it more than mere poetic fancy, for rivers are, in a quite literal sense, boundaries between life and death. If the rivers run dry, then the land becomes a sterile wilderness. It is no surprise to find, for example, that the ancient Egyptians considered the River Nile to be the gift of the god Hapi, for without the annual inundation of the Nile valley, the human settlements of Egypt would, quite simply, cease to exist. Here in Britain we see no such dramatic demonstrations of the absolute necessity of rivers to the life of the land. Yet the necessity exists. The Speaker of the House of Commons, in his address to the Lords in 1655, expressed it in these words: 'Cosmographers do agree that this Island is incomparably furnished with pleasant Rivers, like Veins in the National Body, which convey the Blood into all the Parts, whereby the whole is nourished and made useful.'

A good analogy, for the rivers of Britain are like veins, in that they reach into and nourish all parts of the land, and even the least significant of these rivers has its part to play in the life of the whole.

My own home is in the village of Islip that stands on the banks of the River Ray in Oxfordshire. The relationship between river and settlement is most obvious if you approach the village from the south-east, along what was once the main coaching road from London to Worcester. The road sweeps downhill in a series of wide curves until the last brings a sight of the old stone bridge, flanked at its far end by those twin pillars of rural life: the old rectory with the church tower beyond on one side, the village pub on the other. Behind these, the houses climb the hill forming a tight little settlement, folded in on itself. It is an ancient settlement, for Edward the Confessor was born here, though the cynical might add that nothing of much importance has happened since. The first sight of the village reveals very clearly that the nucleus of it all is the river crossing: the conjunction of highway and river gave birth to the settlement.

The village has clearly changed over the years and is still changing. That change has, in part, been concerned with the river, which has formed a natural boundary to development. Names such as Mill Street are a clear indication that at some time its waters were used to power the local grain mill. Yet surely the river itself is virtually unchanged? If that most pious of English monarchs was to return to his birthplace, would he find the river to be the same? Looking down on the river from the bridge, one would surely think so. Upstream it bends away, bounded on one side by willows and on the other by fields, muddied at the edges where cattle have come to drink. Downstream, it could be a model for one of those famous water paintings by Monet. The weeds stream out in waving parallels beneath the water, trees bend and dip to trail their leaves along the surface and the occasional duck or moorhen is the sole disturber of the scene. Yet if one thought of this as unchanged and unchanging one could not be more mistaken.

To the west of the village, the river passes through the great flat waste of Otmoor. Two centuries ago it was a dreary place of some four thousand acres of wet soil over a clay bed, on which a few sheep and cattle were grazed in summer, though they frequently suffered from rot and a disease known locally as 'moor evil' brought about by standing on the boggy ground. This was common land, and the people in the villages that ring the moor used to send out flocks of geese to feed there. In winter it was covered in flood water and virtually useless. It was, in short, an area where nothing much happened. Indeed, apart from a time centuries ago when the Romans had pushed a road across the moor, nothing much had ever happened—and even the bridge the Romans built soon collapsed, its masonry piling up on the river bed to give the spot the name 'stony ford'. All that changed in the early nineteenth century. The great agriculturist, Arthur Young, in his Report to the Agricultural Board on the state of affairs in the County of Oxfordshire in 1813, wrote: 'I cannot but remark, that such a tract of waste-land in summer, and covered the winter through with water, to remain in such a state, within five miles of Oxford and the Thames, in a kingdom that regularly imports to the amount of a million sterling in corn and is almost periodically visited with apprehensions of want—is a scandal to the national policy.'

Young wished to see the moor drained, enclosed and turned over to agriculture. Two years after his report the work began. To the big landowners it was sound agricultural policy; to the villagers who had the right to graze their few cattle and geese on the moor, it was robbery. There was a popular ballad at the time:

> The fault is great in man or woman,
> That steals a goose from off the common.
> But what can plead that man's excuse,
> That steals the common from the goose?

The villagers attacked the drainage work in every way they could. These were the years of the Otmoor Riots, to be followed by years of legal wrangles, which ended in the 1830s, at which point the local judge breathed a hearty sigh of relief and remarked that he hoped he had heard the last of Otmoor. The drainage work was completed and large parts of the old wasteland were reclaimed. In the process, the River Ray was fundamentally changed. New channels were cut to carry drainage water into the river, the banks were widened and, in places, the stream was diverted into a new, straighter channel. One result of the work can be seen in Islip in very wet weather, when the water draining off the moor swells the river to the point that it overflows its banks. It is not unusual for the Swan Inn to have a real, feathered swan floating past its doorstep. So even in this one quiet spot, one can readily see just how important is the interaction between man and the river which flows through the land on which he has settled.

Although the River Ray is perhaps one of the more extreme examples of a river which has been altered by man, this business of tinkering with the natural waterways is by no means uncommon. In fact, there can scarcely be a river in Britain which man has not tampered with in some way or other. However, long before man began his meddling, the river itself would have established its own path and pattern. So, let us return to a few fundamentals. However much we may romanticize a river, exclaim over its beauties or disclaim on its usefulness, it is, in fact, a drain. The clouds collect over the sea and are blown to the land where they lift and break, allowing the rain to fall to earth. The water sinks into the ground until the ground can take no more and then it collects in pools, large and small, which brim over into rivulets, the

13

rivulets form brooks and streams which trickle down, widen and join to form rivers which run at last to the sea. There, in the heat of the sun, the water evaporates then condenses to form clouds and the cycle is complete.

That is, needless to say, a gross oversimplification of a complex process, but it does emphasize one vital point—the rivers are part of a dynamic, constantly changing system. They can alter from day to day with changes in the weather, and they change again, often quite fundamentally, when looked at over a longer time scale. The river that we saw yesterday is not the same river that we see today. Yet, even so, certain fundamental features remain recognizably the same as far as we, with our short life spans, are concerned, features which depend on the underlying nature of the country through which the river passes. Take, for example, the River Tees which has perhaps the most dramatic changes in character along its path of any river in Britain. It has its origins in the great barren area of Cross Fell, a watershed which sends fast streams down steep narrow valleys to the west, and gives rise to two major rivers in the east—the Tyne and the Tees. The Tees then is only one of a number of rivers having a common origin, but along the way it develops a magnificently dramatic character thanks to a geological formation known as the Whin Sill. Here an igneous rock, that is, one formed by solidification of molten material, has thrust its way between the sedimentary rocks, formed from deposited materials. The softer, sedimentary rocks have been washed away, leaving the hard, igneous rock exposed. The result is, indeed, very like a sill—a sudden rocky drop in the land—and that sill runs right across the line of the Tees. The combination of hard rock sill and river has resulted in two great waterfalls—High Force and Cauldron Snout. Later, the character of the river will change again, meandering out over the plain, snaking and twisting on its way to the sea. The relationship between the nature of the river and the underlying strata may not be so clear elsewhere as it is at the Whin Sill, but it is present all the time.

The river, any river, could be said to have two aspects, both fascinating, and in a way connected. There is the 'natural' river and 'man's' river. This book is mainly concerned with the latter, but the way man deals with the river is determined in the first instance by its natural form. As a prelude, I should like to take a trip down one river from source to mouth to get at least an idea of what this means in practice. I have chosen neither one of the great principal watery veins nor some insignificant side channel, but what one might call a middling river, the Bristol Avon, one of the many Avons with which the country is blessed. The name itself is significant, if in a way rather silly, since if we translate the Celtic half we end up with River River, Avon being no more than the Anglicized version of the Celtic word for river, 'Afon'. Early English settlers hearing the river called Afon kept the name in use. They changed the names of towns and settlements which they took over from Briton or Roman because they wished to establish their own authority, laying claim to what man had made. The river stood outside such narrow interests. It could not be possessed as a house or a village could be possessed, so there was no need to change its name to establish rights of ownership. Afon it had been, and Avon it remained.

The Avon has its origin in water draining off the eastern slopes of the Cotswolds. A ridge of oolitic rock runs in a north-south axis, and this gives shape to the whole river. The westward-draining streams make their way easily to the Bristol Channel, but the Avon has to flow first to the east then, as it clears the ridge, it meanders down to the south before it finds a gap to the west and the sea. The result is a river which doubles right back on itself in a giant U-curve.

It is difficult to say precisely where the river has its source. A number of streams come down from the ridge, of which the most prominent appears round the northern edge of Badminton Park, a spot rather better known to horse lovers than river followers. It turns north by the little village of Luckington, still little more than a stream, but collecting other streams all the while. At Sherston it is met by another major stream, and the two join forces turning off towards the east as something that can reasonably be dignified with the name of 'river'. The village of Sherston itself is still recognizably a part of the Cotswolds, even though we have now moved some way from that long ridge leading off from the main range to the north. The stone is the great mark of the region, that warm Cotswold stone that seems almost to glow in the sunlight. It was used to build all the older houses in the village, which were then topped off by matching stone tiles. The old village sits on the hillside overlooking the river and must, until recently, have formed part of a harmoniously beautiful scene. Looking down from the high ground to the south, the two streams can be seen wandering towards each other, overlooked by the houses clustered round the church tower. That local stone gives to man's creations a feeling of belonging to the scene, as much a proper part of the landscape as the grass, the trees and the river itself. The village, however, has grown, and quarried stone is now an expensive luxury. Modern composites and brick have all but overwhelmed the old. Yet the river still holds its place as a natural boundary, the steep southern slope of the valley effectively blocking off development in that direction. There are also signs here that the river had another role to play, for narrow and shallow though it still is, man was able to find a use for it. The waters were used to turn the wheels of a grain mill that stood by the confluence of the streams.

This stretch of the river is particularly attractive. Although the stream itself is narrow, it has carved a deep valley. The steep, wooded slope and the gently winding river combine in one of those landscapes which were so attractive to eighteenth-century taste, encouraged by fashionable painters and such masterly recreators of landscape as Capability Brown. So, the gentry came and established their house and then proceeded to incorporate the river into the landscaped grounds. Pinkney Park is not one of the great examples of a landscaped garden, but its fresh, natural appearance derives from the same impulse that created the great parks, such as Blenheim. The river was altered to serve the picturesque ideal. Instead of being left to its own devices to wander and tumble where it chose, weirs were constructed. Above the weirs, the river is given extra depth, and the change of level is achieved via a series of charming little waterfalls. At the eastern end, where the parkland meets the tiny hamlet, is a scene of pure enchantment. Upstream, the last of the weirs sparkles with falling water, the steep valley side is rich with trees and flowers, while the minor road is carried across the water on a low bridge with a drystone parapet.

The next river crossing is quite different, an unpaved, dirt road: only the straight line of a route that can be seen stretching, unwavering, to the horizon gives the hint that this is something more than just another country bridlepath. It is, in fact, the Fosse Way, the Roman road arrowing out from Bath to Cirencester and on to Lincoln. River crossings have a special strategic significance and the Fosse Way was, like other Roman roads, part of the military communications set-up of an occupying power. The crossing had to be defended, so a fort was established here, to be followed by a Romano-British settlement. Very little remains to be seen, because the Anglo-Saxons preferred to keep well clear of the main roads. They looked for a defensible position and found just what they wanted a little further down the river at Malmesbury. Here was a site, based on a hill to the north of the river and also bounded by a tributary stream coming down from Tetbury. It is difficult to think of a better example of a site which seemed to cry out for settlement: all around was the fertile plain, watered by the Avon, while the river which helped to create the wealth also formed a barrier against those who might covet it.

Malmesbury can lay claim to being the oldest borough in Britain, having been granted its charter by King Athelstan in the tenth century in gratitude for the brave fight put up by the men of the district against the invading Danes. The original charter has not survived, but it has been copied and renewals by Richard II and William III quote the original. The charter made a good deal of difference to the citizens who were freed from burghbote, brugbote, wardwyte, horngeld and scot. These, which sound as if they might be a set of predatory insects, are the names of a variety of taxes—charges for repairing town walls, charges for bridges, payment for the upkeep of a guard, cattle tax and the customary tax. All this helped to establish Malmesbury as one of the most important towns of the area, and it became home to a splendid monastic foundation.

Malmesbury Abbey has what modern developers would call the prime site in the town, overlooking the river. It was built by the Benedictines in the twelfth century and although only part of it still remains, it is a magnificent example of Romanesque architecture with some remarkably rich carvings, especially those of the south porch. It was also the scene of Britain's first attempted flight by a hang glider. Early in the Abbey's history, a monk by the name of Elmer made wings, which he fastened to his hands and feet. He then proceeded to put them to the test by leaping off the Abbey tower. He glided along for a couple of hundred yards, borne up one suspects as much by his voluminous robes as by the wings, before coming abruptly to earth and breaking both legs. The experiment was not repeated, but a window commemorating the intrepid aviator can be seen in the south wall.

The Abbey is an impressive sight when viewed from the river below the high promontory. From the same spot one can get a lot of hints about the source of later wealth for the town. A little hump-backed bridge crosses the river below the Abbey, and a steep pathway leads up the hill. It could never have been used by carts and waggons, but could easily have been climbed by horses and mules with loads on their backs, the pack animals that carried so much of medieval trade. Beside the bridge are sluice gates, allowing some of the river water to be diverted to turn a water wheel in the mill. So we have trade and a water-powered mill, though little indication of what that trade might be. Look up towards the Abbey and you can see that the trade was probably prosperous, for someone had enough money in the sixteenth century to build themselves a sumptuous house. Abbey House was built, in fact, shortly after the dissolution of the monasteries by Henry VIII, and if you look up the records you will find that it was built by William Stumpe, a local cloth merchant. The equation is complete, the problem solved. Cloth-making lay at the heart of the town's prosperity, and confirmation comes just round the bend of the river with the Avon Mill, an eighteenth-century woollen mill. The river that had begun as the town's defences had now become its major source of power, turning the machinery of industry. This is a theme which is to recur time and time again on our journey down the Avon.

The physical character of the river now changes as it runs into the wide belt of clay that stretches down from Oxford. It is now free to wander where it will, and it proceeds to do just that. No need now to carve a deep passage through the hills, it can meander out into the plain, making great sweeping curves through the water meadows. This is quiet country: no signs of industry, no great foundations, no large towns. It is a landscape of fields and little villages, in which brick from the local clay takes the place of the stone of the Cotswolds. It offers no dramatic surprises nor even any impressive vistas. It is a landscape made for contemplation—unless, of course, you are kept busy, farming the rich land.

The low-lying ground is liable to flooding, a fact which must have been well known to a widow, Maud Heath of Langley Burrell. When she died in 1474, she bequeathed a sum of eighty pounds a year for building and maintaining a road and causeway across the low land. The result can still be seen—Maud Heath's Causeway carried across the river and the surrounding fields on a series of low arches. Not that this was the only, or indeed the earliest, causeway across the river plain. Another went out from Chippenham in the direction of Calne and the upkeep was, in theory at least, paid for by Chippenham. Not that the duty was always taken very seriously; and making one's way through these parts could be a hazardous business, until matters were improved by a great flurry of road improvements in the eighteenth century. For centuries before that, however, the river was a threat to be taken seriously.

Chippenham itself looked to this rich plain for its prosperity as a market town. By now, the river has grown to respectable proportions and modern man has taken new steps to prevent flooding—and thus made the building of long, expensive causeways unnecessary. A large weir has been constructed across the river, with a huge movable gate for flood control. Chippenham is in need of some protection, for it is very low-lying. You can get some idea of how low from the railway which, keeping a level with the surrounding country, runs into the town on a high embankment. Flooding becomes less of a problem as the river moves south, still meandering and twisting on its way, but now cutting a deep channel for itself as it goes. It is pleasant, unpretentious countryside and at one particularly attractive spot, a meadow called Sneylesmede, the Countess of Salisbury founded a nunnery, Lacock Abbey, in 1232. It went the way of all such institutions during the reign of Henry VIII, when it was bought by William Sharington. Fortunately, he was a man of good taste, who incorporated much of the original building into his new house. It changed again over the years after it came into the hands of the Talbot family. John Ivory Talbot had a new entrance built in the eighteenth century, with an extravagant façade in the the then popular Gothic style, considered especially suitable for a former ecclesiastical building. Later Talbots extended the Gothicization of Lacock Abbey.

The most famous inhabitant of the Abbey was William Henry Fox Talbot, the pioneer of photography, whose work is commemorated in a museum next to the house. In 1844, he published a book, *The Pencil of Nature*, which included reproductions of his photographs of his home. The river that ran through the grounds was included, making the Avon the first river ever to be photographed for a book. That river had an important part to play in Abbey life: fish from its waters appeared on the nuns' dinner table, and its clear waters provided them with refreshment. This importance is reflected in the building itself. The vaulted roof of the cloisters boasts some fine carved bosses of the fifteenth century, many of which have watery themes. Up there in the roof are swans and ducks and more fanciful creatures—sea horses, mermaids and mermen. There is one particularly elaborate carving of a large fish holding a rabbit between very toothy jaws. There are also one or two strange-looking humans, whose odd expressions might owe something to another use to which the water could be put—brewing ale. A little brewhouse still stands in a corner of the stable court. It could scarcely be simpler: a circular copper mash tub and boiler in which the malted barley and water were heated mark the beginning of the process. The liquid was then run into a lead-lined cooler and then into a wooden tub, where yeast was added for fermentation. After that it was simply tapped into a container and was ready for use. The virtue of such beer to the presumably sober and pious sisters lay not in its alcoholic content but in its purity. Brewing killed off the germs and bacteria which polluted the natural water source.

Beyond Laycock is Melksham and here the river begins to swing back towards the west, though still keeping within the clay belt. Although the character of the river itself is not changing greatly, it is still growing in power all the time, growing, in fact, to a state where it can support a major industrial complex. This can be seen most clearly in the town which has a good deal to say about the interaction of man and river, Bradford-on-Avon. Approaching the town along the river from the east, no one could have any doubts about the size of the enterprise. Huge mills line the river banks, while great weirs control the flow of water to the wheels that once provided the power. This is the heartland of the once famous West of England woollen industry, where wool from the sheep that grazed the Wiltshire downland was turned into cloth. It was thriving in the seventeenth century, as a number of fine clothiers' houses in the town testify, and it grew in size and importance as the mechanized spinning of the eighteenth century took yarn production away from the home and gave it to the factory. It is a lovely spot and popular with tourists who come to sit and enjoy the pleasant riverside scenery, yet it was that same river which took Bradford into the factory age when the other Bradford in Yorkshire was little more than a hamlet. The river provided the power for the new machines. Those were the years when today's quiet, picturesque tourist spot was a battleground as the old generation of hand-loom weavers and spinners fought a desperate and doomed action against the changes that would transform their lives.

The town has, of course, a history that goes back far beyond the industrial revolution. Flemish weavers came here as early as the fourteenth century, when a settlement had already been established based on the importance of the river crossing. The bridge also dates back to the fourteenth century, but has been much altered. A small chapel for travellers to give thanks for a safe crossing was built into the fabric, though a less religious age found other uses for the building. It was adapted in the seventeenth century to serve as a lock-up, and, as most of its inhabitants were the town drunks, it became known locally as the Blind House. It did, however, house one religious prisoner, when John Wesley was locked up for his non-conformist preaching. He spent the night, it is said, in converting the warder.

The river flows on through this once busy industrial town, wide and deep, but not yet deep enough to act as a transport route for the mills and factories. Water transport came, not on the river, but on the Kennet and Avon Canal which, from here to Bath, is a close neighbour to the river. The essential nature of a canal demands that it keep, as far as possible, to one level, and the steep-sided valley of the Avon provided a less than ideal terrain for the canal's engineer, John Rennie. He found the river to be both friend and enemy. Beyond Bradford, the river is again faced by that same tongue of oolitic rock from which it had its origin. It cuts a passage through, but the result is this very narrow, steep-sided valley. Rennie would have liked to run his canal along one side of the valley, keeping to a level all the way, but he was not able to achieve that ideal. Instead, he was forced to swing his artificial waterway from one side of the valley to the other, twice crossing the river on stone aqueducts. The first is at Avoncliff, but the grander of the two is two miles further on, the Dundas aqueduct.

The conjunction of river and canal is by no means unique, but there are few places where the work of the engineers is seen to better effect. There are a number of spectacular aqueducts carrying artificial canals across natural rivers, providing the extraordinary sight of boats sailing high above the tops of trees—at Marple over the Goyt, at Lancaster over the Lune, over the Almond near Edinburgh and, supremely, over the Dee near Llangollen. Yet if one is looking for a sense of style, there is nothing quite to match Dundas. Classicism was all the rage in Georgian Britain and, no doubt encouraged by the fact that he was now close to that most perfect of Georgian cities, Bath, Rennie took the classical style and adapted it to the demands of civil engineering. He used the rich, honey-coloured Bath stone for building, a stone which deserves to be bathed in perpetual sunlight. Where some materials hold up hard faces to the sun, throwing it back in a dazzling glare, Bath stone seems to absorb it and then emit it anew as a softly glowing radiance. The beauty of the stone matches the style. A single arch crosses the river, balanced by smaller arches to the side. Doric columns decorate the aqueduct, which is topped by a deep cornice and a balustrade. The effect of water crossing water always has something strange about it, but here where everything is carried off with such panache and where the background is a beautiful wooded valley, the strangeness is less obvious than the pure enchantment.

The river winds on its way, with the canal keeping pace alongside but above it. A frequent problem faced by all canal engineers was that of finding water to fill their canals and keep them filled. John Rennie had the river close at hand, but some fifty feet below. How was he to get the water up the hillside? His ingenious answer was to let the river itself do the work for him. At Claverton, the Canal Company took over the site of a water mill and built a pumping station. There they installed a nineteen-foot-wide water wheel which was used to provide the power for a pair of beam pumps. So, river water is lifted by the power of river water, a satisfyingly elegant solution to a problem.

The river is more than just a barrier or a source of power. Its physical characteristics have given shape to man's work. The narrowness of the valley has forced generations of engineers to adapt their routes to fit its awkward shape. The main road from Bath to Salisbury, the Kennet and Avon Canal, the Great Western Railway, all huddle together, following the river as it curves round in a great S-bend that eventually brings it to the city of Bath.

The city is mainly contained within the bend of the river as it comes in from the east, swings round to the south and then heads off again to the west. It is, of course, famous for its hot springs. Such springs may be a commonplace in some parts of the world, but they are a rarity in Britain and were held in special reverence for centuries before the Romans came and established Aquae Sulis, erecting a temple to Sul Minerva. But it was the Romans who turned a natural curiosity into the basis for a beautiful city. The greatest hydraulic engineers of the ancient world, they tamed the springs to serve their baths, which were a cross between a modern spa and a holy place. You could immerse yourself in order to cure rheumatism, or throw in an offering to the gods, who might cure you without your ever having to get wet at all. You could ask for curses on enemies as well as blessings on friends. A small lead plaque has been discovered which asks the gods to make the suppliant's enemy 'as liquid as water'. Someone had stolen his lover, who seemed to have been less than constant in her affections, since the curser was uncertain which of nine possible contenders deserved liquefaction. He played safe by cursing them all.

The Romans controlled both springs and flood waters, but as the Roman Empire crumbled away into the Dark Ages, so the city itself crumbled and the area returned to a swampy waste. Bath's second great period of glory came in the eighteenth and early nineteenth century, when the spa became the most fashionable spot in all Britain. It remains, in spite of the worst efforts of developers and council, the most perfect of Georgian cities and that sense of grace and elegance extends to the river. The bridges in the Bath area provide a fascinating commentary on this particular aspect of engineering history.

The story begins properly on the outskirts of the city, at Bathampton. Road building in the eighteenth century was largely a matter for private enterprise. A Turnpike Trust was formed which would collect money to pay for a new road, and would then expect to make a profit by charging tolls to the road users. A similar system operated with bridges. The Bathampton Bridge, which carries a cross road linking the major roads out of Bath, is still privately owned and still has its toll house where travellers pay their dues. Otherwise, it is a pleasant but unremarkable stone structure. Such a description would certainly not fit Bath's most famous bridge. Pulteney Bridge was designed in 1771 by that great architect Robert Adam and it is, rather surprisingly, the only example of his work in the city. He based his design on the Ponte Vecchio in Florence. It is built in Bath stone and both sides of the bridge are lined with shops, so that those using the bridge are scarcely aware that they are crossing the river at all. But seen from the river bank, its beauty is revealed. Nineteenth-century bridge builders often turned away from traditional materials and traditional methods. Victoria Bridge is a suspension bridge built in 1836 to a unique design, patented by J. Dredge. The suspension rods in Dredge's design slope in towards the stone piers. It is not perhaps one of the world's great bridges but it says something about the growing taste for experimentation among Victorian engineers.

Bath marks an important turning point in the story of the river. Here canal and river meet. The artificial waterway is no longer needed, for the river itself is now navigable. Yet the river has to be controlled. It is no longer permitted to make its own way where it will, and its course to Bristol is governed by weirs and artificial cuttings. Where there would have been a steady fall, there is now the abrupt drop at the weir with boats being diverted into artificial channels and raised or lowered by means of locks. Vessels up to seventy-five-foot long and sixteen-foot beam can travel the route to Bristol, and it soon becomes apparent that there would have been no shortage of customers for the old working boatmen. The region was, until recently, the centre of a thriving brass and copper industry, which used the river as a source of power. The typical building of the brass industry is the annealing oven, generally a tall, tapering structure of a type which can be seen at the river side at the old Kelston works between Saltford and Swineford. There were no fewer than six water wheels here, powering the various slitting and cutting machines. This now peaceful stretch of the river was as busy as any in the country, though it is difficult to imagine the scene. Furnaces flared and smoked on both banks; water wheels rumbled to turn the machines while the river itself was busy with boats carrying raw materials and finished products. Most of those products finished up at Bristol, to be sent out to the rest of Britain and, indeed, to the rest of the world.

Until the end of the eighteenth century, Bristol was Britain's second most important port, after London. The Avon was wide and deep enough to take the biggest sea-going vessels and could provide a safe anchorage. It looked first to a trade with Europe and then, in later days, towards North America. It gained fresh riches in the eighteenth century as the centre for the infamous slave trade. Boats set out on a triangular route: trade goods were sent to Africa where they were exchanged for slaves, who were then taken to America where they were, in turn, exchanged for rum, tobacco and sugar. For centuries, the river had proved adequate to all the demands of trade, but as ships became larger so the demands for improved facilities grew. Bristol was slow to respond to a threat from the north-west and the rapidly developing port of Liverpool. New docks were finally put in hand at the end of the eighteenth century when William Jessop was brought in to design a floating harbour, one where ships could safely float at all states of the tide. A new channel was cut, controlled by lock gates, and the river itself diverted into the New Cut. Extra water for the harbour was brought in by means of a feeder canal. The work was completed in 1809 and the river scene in Bristol today is substantially the result of Jessop's work. It was a major achievement, a fine piece of civil engineering, but it came too late. Liverpool had taken the lead, and was not about to let go. There was a last valiant attempt to restore Bristol's flagging fortunes by Isambard Kingdom Brunel. He tried to establish the port as the base for a new transatlantic steamer service, and the SS *Great Britain* has been brought back to the city where it was launched as a reminder of those exciting days. The revival attempt failed. Today the river has little traffic and the Victorian warehouses, built in the grandiose style known as Bristol Byzantine, are all that remain, faded reminders of a glorious past.

Bristol owed its importance, however, to more than its overseas trade. It stands near the confluence of two major rivers: the Avon itself and the far more important Severn, while another comparatively minor navigable river, the Wye, joins in nearby. The port was thus the natural centre for a complex of internal trade routes: up the Severn to Bewdley and, in medieval times, beyond that and into the Stratford Avon; along the Wye to Wales and across the Bristol Channel to South Wales. Through the port of Bristol came the busy import-export traffic that linked the sea routes to the interior, and there was a busy internal trade as well. Agricultural produce from Wales bound for the industrial Midlands was as important a feature of river traffic as sugar from the West Indies or wine from France. Until the age of railways, river transport was the best and most efficient way of moving bulky goods around the country. Even in the railway age itself, the port was still considered to have an important role to play. Brunel conceived a great plan for a transport system that would link London with New York. His Great Western Railway would carry passengers from Paddington to Bristol, where his steamships would take them down the river and out on to the high seas. It was a bold plan that came very close to success.

Beyond Bristol, the river achieves its most spectacular effect, carving a deep gorge through the limestone ridge at Clifton. Here, at least, man has combined with nature to make a splendid scene even more memorable. The gorge is crossed by Brunel's famous suspension bridge. The story of this much praised, and justly praised, structure is long and complex and will be told in detail later in the book (see p. 129), but it is worthwhile pausing in our imaginary trip along the river to consider the implications of this bridge. It is all too easy to underestimate the complexities of a problem if one happens to know the answer already. It is rather like playing solitaire, an infuriating game that keeps one baffled for hours on end, but once you have it solved you wonder where the difficulty lay. So it is with the bridge. But just imagine what it must have meant to stand on the brink of that great cleft before it was spanned. The task must have seemed Herculean, yet the answer found by Brunel is so simple, so very elegant. Later engineers have built longer bridges, higher bridges, even more spectacular bridges but there are none which better epitomize the daring and ingenuity of a great man.

At last, the river reaches its destination at Avonmouth and the broad waters of the Severn estuary. Here is the new port that handles the giant ships of the second half of the twentieth century—the container vessels, the tankers and the supertankers. The stream that trickled down the Cotswold slopes has at last emerged as a wide river, where the fresh water from the land mingles with the salt water from the sea. Throughout its long journey one can see how its presence has affected man. It has made his fields fertile, served as a source of power, provided a barrier to other transport routes while itself providing a useful route for boatmen. Settlements formed along its banks date back to prehistory. The river helped to determine how men lived their lives, and men in their turn changed the river to suit their needs. The same process can be seen at work on all the major rivers of the country, and no river is so insignificant as not to have had some part to play in human history. This book is about that complex relationship between man and the

25

rivers, but perhaps it is worth remembering that this is a very egocentric view. The rivers have an existence of their own which is quite independent of our short stay on this planet, and we are by no means the only life form to depend on them. Animals, fish, birds, insects, plants—all have as great a claim on the rivers as we have. And that too is part of the river story, for it is only recently that we have come back to an awareness of a fundamental truth. We, too, are part of the whole wide order of nature, and we disregard that order at our peril.

CHAPTER TWO

Down to the valleys

Rivers existed before man came and will, no doubt, continue to exist after he has gone. We know little of the days when man first came to these islands and little too about what kind of land he found. When we look back into the distant past and try to picture the scene, it is rather as if we had been presented with a vast and complex jigsaw from which someone has unkindly removed the majority of the pieces. The archaeological evidence that survives might suggest certain theories, but there is always a lingering suspicion that what has not survived might have contradicted them. But all the time, new techniques are being brought in to expand our notions of the past. For example, Professor Geoffrey Dimbleby of the Institute of Archaeology at London University has recently shown how the study of plant remains can yield valuable evidence. He has suggested that mesolithic man used fire to prevent the upward spread of the forests in the Pennines, which brings us to the first rough generalization. Early settlement took place on the uplands, not down in the river valleys.

How did early man regard the rivers? One's first reaction is to answer—with considerable dismay. Those valleys were thickly forested, choked with vegetation and even if the ground could be cleared, the soil was usually too heavy to be turned by any plough he could devise. So he turned instead to the thin soil of the uplands. Quite when man gave up the nomadic life of hunter and food-gatherer we do not know, but the oldest recognizable system of cornfields and accompanying stone huts dates from the early Bronze Age, perhaps 2000 to 1500 BC. They are found in the south-west, on the edges of Dartmoor and Bodmin Moor in Cornwall. The lowland areas, the river valleys, remained virtually uninhabitable for a very long time, but that does not mean that early man found no use at all for the rivers that crossed the land.

The most magnificent monument of the ancient world in Britain is undoubtedly Stonehenge on Salisbury Plain. Why Stonehenge was built some time in the Neolithic period—the actual construction coming in two phases, the first around 2600 BC, the second some two centuries later—is not our concern here. The interesting question to ask is how the stones came to the site. The bluestones, each weighing around four tons, were brought from the Prescelly Mountains in Pembrokeshire. Several theories have been put forward as to how this was achieved, including a number of recent suggestions involving men from space and flying saucers. Such theories cannot be disproved, but there seems little point in opting for the improbable when we have the possible close at hand. The most likely explanation is that they were brought around the coast and then up the Wiltshire Avon. In a trial of the theory, a simple raft was constructed and a two-ton stone lowered on board. It was found that this crude craft could easily be poled along by a couple of schoolboys and that it would float in very shallow water. If this is the true explanation then long before man settled beside the rivers, he was already seeing them as a convenient highway.

When did all this begin? When did man first realize that floating along a river was an excellent method of moving from place to place? Here there is very little direct evidence from Britain, but we can find plenty of evidence in other parts of the world to indicate how man got around in the water. Man is a natural swimmer. Place a few-weeks-old baby in water and it will float. Unfortunately, we lose the knack after those first few weeks, but even if we do relearn the skills we are poor performers. Even the finest athletes do not rate particularly well in terms of the animal world as a whole, so, at a very early stage, man started looking around for artificial aids. As the incentive for getting in the water in the first place was the desire to catch fish or carry some object across, there was a need to keep at least one hand free. Various forms of floats were used, including quite unsophisticated devices such as inflated animal skins. An Assyrian sculpture of the ninth century BC shows warriors using such floats to cross a river—and, in 1980, newspapers carried photographs of modern warriors using identical devices in northern India.

The simplest float is probably a piece of wood, which the swimmer rests under his armpits, but that is both clumsy and very uncomfortable. A logical development would be to combine pieces of wood to form a raft, and possibly to add bladders as floats. One other obvious method of floating is to find a log and sit on it but, as most of us discovered as children, the end result of this unstable method is a ducking. If, however, you hollow out your log and stop up the ends, then you have a dug-out canoe, a genuine boat, and remains of such simple vessels have been found in different parts of Britain. The problem with the dug-out canoe is that its manufacture requires tools and a good deal of hard labour. So rather than start with a solid material and laboriously hack it into shape, why not start with a light, pliable material and build up your boat from that? Such boats were in regular use in the Middle East in ancient times, the earliest recorded traveller in such a vessel perhaps being the infant Moses, floating in a watertight basket among the reeds of the Nile. Many varieties of boats were built in this way—papyrus rafts, reed boats and giant basket-like vessels known as qaffas. And such a vessel was in use in Britain before the Roman conquest. It was the coracle.

Julius Caesar in his campaign against Pompey in 49 BC found that his lines of communication across the River Segre had been cut by the demolition of a bridge. He then ordered his troops to build boats of the type he had seen in Britain during the campaign of 56–55 BC. The boats as he described them to his troops had keels and ribs of light wood filled in with wickerwork. The whole was then covered with hide. The Roman coracles were a success, and the army was safely ferried across. Many Roman writers refer to coracles, including Pliny, who mentions coracles from Cornwall taking tin to the Isle of Wight, which was presumably a staging post on the route to Europe. Coracle-type boats were, in fact, known throughout the British Isles. The Scots used a comparatively primitive form of coracle on the Spey, and share with the Irish a tradition of long voyages by hide-covered boats. The most famous of these was the voyage reputed to have been made to North America by St Brendan in a large boat of this type, the curragh. A recent expedition, using a curragh built as it might have been in the sixth century when St Brendan was alive, showed that whether or not it did actually occur, such a voyage was technically possible. The coracle, however, is something more than a folk memory and a few references in ancient texts, for coracle building has continued right down to the present day.

It is not difficult to see why the coracle has remained a practical vessel in spite of two thousand and more years of improvement in boat design. Firstly, it is very light. The coracle owner can pick up his vessel, sling it on his back and walk down to the river looking rather like a two-legged tortoise. Once in the water, the coracle has one major disadvantage, at least as far as those uninitiated in its use are concerned; the beginner generally finds that the best he can achieve is a giddy, spinning motion with the little craft whirling round in circles. But, in the hands of the experienced boatman, it is a very manoeuvrable craft, which has the great advantage that it can be propelled by a single oar held in one hand. The blade of the oar is kept permanently in the water, and the boat is moved along by a figure-of-eight motion of the blade. This makes it possible, for example, for two boatmen to go out on the river and hold a fishing net between the vessels.

The British coracle has changed over the years, but in its essentials it is still recognizable as the craft that impressed Julius Caesar. In shape, it is more or less rectangular, with a flattened bow and almost semi-circular stern. It has a very shallow draught, which makes it ideal for fast, rocky rivers, such as those of South Wales. It is in such areas that the coracle has remained in use, with occasional survivors on the border river, the Severn. By the seventeenth century, the hide cover had been replaced by flannel, a product of the Welsh woollen industry. This, in turn, was later replaced by cotton, in both cases the cloth being coated with tar. It is a happy thought for traditionalists that this earliest recorded form of native British craft is not only still in use, but is finding a new popularity among sportsmen. Many canoe clubs now include coracles among the more familiar kayaks.

At the time of the Roman invasion, the British were making extensive use of their rivers, but still based their settlements on high ground, with huts grouped around a hill fort. Yet already there were changes, the pattern was being broken. Groups of settlers from Northern Europe, the Belgae, had begun to move into England. Their tribal centres were a complete contrast to the British forts. They sought safety in clearings cut from the thick forest, preferably beside a small river or stream. They relied on the dense forest and the marshland to protect them. The country was divided between two quite separate regions and two quite separate cultures. There were the uplands where living was hard and was literally scratched out of the earth as the primitive ploughs cut into the shallow, poor soil. The people were hardy and obdurate and were to remain comparatively untouched by Romanism. The Romans, in fact, soon gave up the attempt to come to terms with them and simply shunted them off to the more remote mountainous regions, keeping them there, where necessary, by defensive barriers such as Hadrian's Wall. The lowlanders were very different. They had settled those areas which they could make habitable, though some of the thickly forested regions such as the Weald remained impenetrable. They found their ideal in areas such as the gravel beds of the Thames valley, very accessible land for farming. These people responded to the new civilization imported from the Mediterranean, using the new techniques and the new technology of Rome. Rivers were now to play an important role in the land: new settlements would appear along

Above: A medieval mixed fishery. Above the bridge, orthodox rod and line; below, netting and naked pursuit.

Right: A successful medieval float-fisherman, from a contemporary woodcut.

Above: A medieval mining scene with ore crushers powered by water following techniques introduced by the Romans.

Right: An example of the use of water power from a German treatise of 1617.

their banks, impressive bridges would be thrown across their waters and those same waters would be put to use. But before any of that could happen, there was to be a dramatic demonstration of one other aspect of rivers—their military significance. It appeared in the Battle of the Medway.

Caesar's two expeditions had not been aimed specifically at conquest, but were more in the nature of punitive raids. Rome's main concern was with continental Europe, but the Gaulish leaders had begun to use Britain as a safe retreat, where they could pause to gather strength before the next round of battle. The British expeditions were inconclusive, and the British leaders were not convinced of the invincibility of Roman force. After Caesar's campaigns there was something of a lull in Britain while Rome attended to more pressing matters in Europe. The British problem was shelved but not forgotten, and inevitably the time came when Rome began to think of conquest.

The invasion of 43 AD was intended as a triumph for Claudius. It was generally thought that there would be little trouble in completing the campaign, and an army was sent under Plautius with the general idea that, after a softening-up period, Claudius himself would come over and take charge of the decisive phase. He was rather in need of a popular triumph just then. There were good reasons for supposing that the campaign would be brief and not unduly taxing. Britain was still very much a tribal society, and the one strong leader who might have organized a concerted opposition, Cunobelinus, was dead. His two sons, Togodommius and Caratacus took up the leadership, but there was little coordination among their forces. At first the British simply vanished in front of the Roman forces who were spoiling for a fight but quite unable to find anyone to fight with. Then the British made their move, a phrase which perhaps suggests something more planned and better organized than was in fact the case. The two sons simply led their followers down in a rush, and the well-organized Roman troops had no difficulty in turning back the disorganized mob. Caratacus fled and, rather late in the day, sat down to think up a rational plan. He decided to take up a defensible position and make a stand on the Medway.

The British forces of foot soldiers and very mobile chariots retreated across the river, destroying the primitive bridge behind them. There they felt secure, certain that they had the only possible crossing point controlled. They had underestimated Roman resourcefulness. The foot soldiers found a fording point upstream, while the cavalry swam the river lower down. The British forces were taken by surprise and completely ouflanked. The pattern

31

of British battles in the past had been one of quick headlong dashes at the enemy, followed by equally rapid retreats. Here things were to be different. The Medway had been chosen as the one defensible line, and Caratacus was determined to defend it. The battle lasted for two whole days and at the end the Romans were the victors. All British hopes had been fastened on the Medway defence and when that fell the way was open to the advancing Romans.

Shakespeare sets the crucial battle in the time of Cunobelinus (Cymbeline) and ends his play with a fine patriotic fervour, with Rome and Britain united as equal allies, marching to a glorious future.

> Publish we this peace
> To all our subjects. Set we forward: let
> A Roman and a British ensign wave
> Friendly together; so through Lud's town march;
> And in the temple of great Jupiter
> Our peace we'll ratify; seal it with feasts.
> Set on there. Never was a war did cease,
> Ere bloody hands were wash'd, with such a peace.

The rhetoric is more impressive than the historical accuracy. There was no equal partnership: Britain was to become a Roman province, paying tribute to Rome. Nor was there an immediate and final peace. Yet the feeling that the Medway Battle represents a beginning as well as an end is real enough. Britain was to absorb a good deal of both the culture and technology of Rome.

Perhaps the most notable feature of the Roman occupation is the establishment of towns and cities which have, in many cases, maintained their importance right through to modern times. There are two factors which helped to determine the siting of these settlements. The first derived from the colonial nature of Roman rule: the centre of power and wealth was Rome, and Rome could only be reached by crossing the sea. Major centres, therefore, needed this access to the sea. As a subsidiary to this requirement, the centres also needed to be points from which the surrounding countryside could be controlled. Place your administrative centre on the coast and you automatically reduce the area of control, since on one side you have the sea, rather than the populated land. There were therefore great advantages in establishing such centres away from the coast, but on navigable rivers with access to the sea. The second criterion related to what must be the best known of all the characteristics of the Roman Empire—its roads. The

Roman road is perhaps the most extraordinary manifestation of the Roman genius for organization and egocentricity. The two, no doubt, go together: one needs to be totally self-centred to pursue an objective ruthlessly, quite unconcerned with all subsidiary issues. If the Romans wanted a road from A to B, then from A to B it went, regardless of what lay in between. Yet this very directness and the high quality of the highway made them vulnerable. The roads were so excellent that an army forced to take a different route was at a serious disadvantage. So strategic points along the way had to be guarded, and no points had greater significance than the river crossings. So, if one combines the value of access to the sea with a river crossing, you have the basis for an important centre. This combination occurs at York, Chester, Lincoln, Gloucester, Colchester and, of course, London. These were the major cities although, by today's standards, they seem small enough. Even the largest, London, contained little more than three hundred acres within its walls. The next level down, as it were, were the towns that developed out of forts. Occasionally these continued to keep their traditional identity for a very long time. Catterick, for example, derived its name from the Latin original, which in turn owed its origins to the cataracts on the River Swale. The names survived, as did the military connection at Catterick Camp. The essential point about all these settlements, however, is their location which owed nothing to the existing British settlements but did owe a great deal to the presence of the rivers.

The Romans looked towards the continent for two reasons: to keep communications open with their home base and for trade. As time went on, trade became ever more important. A Britain that had previously only seen the humble coracle on its waters was now given the sight of very much grander vessels. The remains of a Roman merchant ship were recovered from the mud of the Thames near Westminster Bridge in 1910. It was incomplete, but we can surmise a great deal about the original. It was built at some time in the third century and was quite a large vessel, around sixty foot long. It was carvel-built, that is to say the planks abut each other to form a smooth surface, as opposed to clinker-built vessels where the planks overlap. These planks were held together by wooden pegs, known as tree-nails. The hull itself was constructed around a framework of wooden ribs, set a foot or so apart. Its overall shape is not completely clear, but contemporary illustrations show merchant vessels with rounded stems, with two quarter rudders for steering and sharply beaked bows. The single mast carried a square sail, which made it difficult to do much beyond running before a following wind.

There was a certain amount of manoeuvrability to windward, but not a great deal, though such vessels could easily cross the Channel to London. As well as these sea-going vessels, the Romans built barges for river work. These carried several oars on each side, though in hull design they were often very similar to the ocean-going vessels. Remains are few, simply because wood rots, but we know from contemporary accounts and illustrations that there was extensive barge traffic throughout the Roman Empire, including Britain.

Rivers were, for many centuries, the cheapest means of moving goods around the country, and were of major importance in the development of trade. To the inland navigators they were a boon, but to the overland traveller and the road builder they were an expensive nuisance. Roman bridge building was of a magnificently high standard, but we have no way of knowing how much better it was than its predecessors. The earliest type of bridge would appear to be the clapper bridge, such as Tarr Steps on Exmoor or Postbridge on Dartmoor, where slabs of stone have simply been dropped on to piles of smaller stones to form the bridge. Unfortunately, we have no means of dating these structures. They might be very early: equally they might be no more than a cheap and simple local response to a purely local problem, in which case they could be medieval or even later. Such bridges could, in any case, only be built over shallow rivers. They are, when all is said and done, little better than sophisticated stepping stones. The bridge across which Caratacus fled over the Medway must have been a very different structure. Whatever form it took, it would have been unlikely to have influenced the Roman engineers who brought their own sophisticated and well-tried ideas with them. Just how sophisticated those ideas could be can be seen from surviving bridges in Europe, of which one of the finest is the first-century bridge over the Marecchia. Perhaps the greatest compliment one can pay to such a bridge is to say that one would not be in the least surprised to be told that it had been built a thousand or more years later. The river is crossed by five semi-circular stone arches, and it is embellished with all those details which were to be copied in more modern times during the classical revival, such as niches between the arches and a dentilled cornice. Purely engineering innovations include the cutwaters on the upstream side: these are shaped stones placed between the arches to ease the flow of water through the bridge.

Nothing like a complete Roman bridge has survived in Britain. There are, however, two bridges across the River Rede, a tributary of the Tyne, close to the fort of Chesters on Hadrian's Wall. The more substantial of the two had four arches, each over thirty-five feet wide, and the piers had cutwaters on the upstream side. Since it was built, the river has shifted in its course, so that the western abutments have disappeared under water. At the opposite end of the bridge, the eastern abutment has been left high and dry and open to inspection. This was certainly no gimcrack construction. It was built of massive stone blocks, each carefully dressed by the mason and equally carefully fitted to its neighbour. A phallus has been carved on one of the stones, presumably as a good luck emblem rather than as a casual graffito left by a bored legionary. The platform was possibly of wood, with a drawbridge mechanism. It all indicates a fine structure, but within the tower is an indication of an even more exciting technical innovation. An extra channel has been cut, through which water was diverted and used to turn a water wheel.

If we think of advances in technology as a slow, steady climb up a long flight of stairs then, with the Roman occupation, the British found themselves leaping over several steps at a single bound. After the Romans left, their roads fell into decay and many of their manufacturing secrets were lost. Great towns became ruins and the stones were robbed for humbler settlements, while the statues of the gods and the temples made way for the ikons of a new religion. Yet this one technical advance remained. Man had acquired a source of power greater than that of his own arms or his horse and oxen, and he did not relinquish that power. The introduction of the water wheel began a period of water power usage which was to continue and to grow right up to the nineteenth century. It is not too fanciful to think of the water wheel as perhaps the most valuable legacy of Roman rule.

The common water wheel that we know has a vertical wheel fitted with paddles and turns around a horizontal axis. It is sometimes known as the Vitruvian wheel, after Vitruvius who first gave an accurate description of such a device in his book, *De Architectura*, written around 15 BC. Not that this was the earliest known reference to a water wheel, but where Vitruvius' is a straightforward technical description, that of Antipotas of Thessalonica, writing over half a century earlier, is quite lyrical: 'Ease your labours, you who labour at the mill. Sleep, and leave the birds to sing to the blood red dawn. Ceres has commanded the water nymphs to do your work. Obeying her call, they throw themselves at the wheel to turn the axle and the mill.'

The water wheel is capable of development into an immensely powerful machine, but in Rome it was not taken up with any marked or immediate enthusiasm. Thanks to the spread of the Empire, Rome was well endowed with thousands of slaves, and what would they do if machines did the work for them? As far as one can tell, this is the first recorded example of a now familiar problem of technological advance. Today we worry about the silicon chip: then it was the water wheel. Nevertheless, the water wheel did come into use, though it did not represent the most dramatic example of the Romans' ability to use the rivers of Britain for industry. The country is comparatively rich in minerals. There were, for example, extensive Roman lead mines both in Derbyshire and the Mendips. There was also mining in Wales, where the Romans found veins of the precious metal, gold.

Once you have located gold, you can work it by first removing the overburden, soil and loose stone and then, when the veins of ore have been revealed they can be followed underground. At the Roman gold mines of Dolaucothi, near the village of Pumpsaint in mid-Wales, the Romans found gold in the hillside, but before work could begin on burrowing into the hill, there was a good deal of top surface to be removed, and they employed a technique known as 'hushing'. Water was sent rushing in torrents down the hillside to wash away the topsoil and reveal the ore-bearing rock underneath. There was, however, one minor problem to overcome: how to get water to the top of the hill in the first place. If there was one skill which the Romans were acknowledged masters of, then that skill was in hydraulic engineering. Down in the valley, the little Afon Cothi winds its way past the village, where the Romans established their fort, together with a strong-room for the gold they hoped to win. A second river, the Anwell, runs nearby. Now, as water will always run downhill, all the Romans had to do, in theory, was to trace the rivers back to a point where they were at a greater altitude than the mine and then divert the water down an artificial channel or aqueduct. The theory could not be simpler, but the practical problems were immense. When the miners reached the appropriate height on the Cothi, they discovered they were seven miles away from the main site. Yet they still went ahead and constructed their aqueduct and above the mine itself they dug huge reservoirs to hold the water. The aqueduct system of shallow channels can still be seen on the hills around Dolaucothi and the great reservoirs with their thick earth banks remain as dips and hollows in the hillside. It requires a little imagination to imagine the scene when the reservoirs were opened and thousands of gallons of water poured down the steep hillside, stripping it to the hard rockface. The whole project was carried out on a massive scale, and if one wanted an example of what Roman

36

technology meant to Britain one could hardly find a better spot to visit.

Man's relationship to the rivers went through a fundamental change during the Roman period, though the change was at first limited to England and small parts of Scotland and Wales. To the Roman, the river was there to be used. As he established his towns and villages throughout the country-side, he applied quite different criteria from those that had prevailed in the old Britain of warring tribes and factions. The troublesome natives were pushed to the extremities, behind the artificial boundaries of Hadrian's and the Antonine Walls, and the natural boundaries formed by the Wye, Severn and Tamar. Within the rest of the country, the legions could ensure peace and the land could be settled. Once the forest and thick vegetation had been cleared, then the river valley made the ideal setting for a new villa. The Roman settler looked for a site with a south-facing slope, in the hope if not the expectation of capturing some of the warmth of the sun that would have been one of the pleasures of life back home in Italy. The water of the river could be diverted to serve the new house. The huge aqueduct system of Dolaucothi was reproduced in miniature a thousand times over for the more mundane, but no less important, task of supplying domestic water. The bath house, without which no respectable Roman would consider a settlement civilized, demanded a constant supply of running water, and aqueducts were built from the nearest river which could supply it. A very fine example of this type of work can be seen in Dorset. A canal was dug from the River Frome, near Maiden Newton, and it meandered along, following the contours of the land, all the way to Dorchester.

The idea of artificial cuttings being joined to rivers found an even wider application in the fenland of East Anglia. There, instead of taking water from the river to serve the land, the cuttings were used to drain water off the land into the river. The finest example is the Car Dyke, which joins the Nene near Peterborough to the Witham near Lincoln, a total length of fifty-six miles. A shorter section of dyke with the same name joins the Cam to the Ouse. Vast areas of swamp were drained and brought under cultivation, and the drainage dykes added considerably to the water flowing down the East Anglian rivers. The dykes themselves might also have been used for transport. One certainly was, and still is, used by boats, the Foss Dyke, connecting the wide waters of the tidal Trent to Lincoln and the Witham. This connection had enormous importance for the development of Lincoln and the port of Boston. It joined together two major river systems, and through these made connections to the Midlands in one direction and as far north as York in the other. Just how many of the drainage dykes were navigable is uncertain, but it is certainly true that, thanks to Roman initiative, the rivers and dykes of East Anglia were to enjoy a prosperous water trade that lasted for many centuries.

Roman rule, then, brought change to the whole face of Britain, and nowhere was this more apparent than in the river valleys. The newcomers showed little interest in draughty hill forts and the legions who had to do their stint on the wind-swept uplands regarded such postings as a form of punishment. Civilization was to be found in the valleys. But Roman rule and Roman ways were not to last for ever. Decay set in at the very heart of the Empire, in Rome itself. The Empire collapsed and the British portion fell with the rest. There was no sudden catastrophe: Rome and civilization one day, barbarians and the Dark Ages the next. Links with Rome were severed when the last of the legions crossed the Channel in 406. After that, when local leaders appealed to Rome for help against the raids that were threatening from all directions, the Emperor Honorius offered them no hope. Rome could no longer defend itself, let alone care for a distant outpost. In 410 the Visigoths were marching in the streets of Rome.

In Britain, the old civil administration creaked on for a long while, but the machinery of government was wearing out and the day was to come when it would seize up altogether. Meanwhile, thanks to Roman efforts, Britain had become a desirable residence with vacant possession for many would-be occupants. The Picts raided into Scotland and staked their claims, the Irish attacked from the west and there was a strong flow of immigrants from across the North Sea. The latter were, at first, the Saxon mercenaries who had lost a paymaster, and who sent word back to their kin that here was a land worth taking. They came across the Channel in large numbers and their boats were soon to be seen travelling up the rivers of southern England. We know something of these ships from the famous Sutton Hoo burial. Here, the body of a chieftain was buried, together with his treasures, in a fine Saxon ship. These ships seem to have been from sixty to eighty feet long, propelled by some thirty oarsmen. There is no sign of any stepping for a mast, so it seems probable that no sail was used. The vessel was clinker-built, the overlapping fifteen-inch planks being lashed to the ribs. Such vessels were capable of travelling considerable distances upriver for, although they were five feet deep, they only drew two feet of water. They were serviceable vessels, even if they represented little if any improvement over the Roman ships.

For a time there was resistance, but the contemporary Gallic Chronicle describes how the newcomers 'brought by the strength of oarsmen and the blowing wind, broke through the boundaries and spread slaughter on every side'. There was a stern British resistance led by Arthur, an historical figure of considerable stature, but one who had very little in common with the mythical figure of later stories and legends. Gradually, the British were pushed back, yet again, to the highlands, forming enclaves in Scotland, Wales and the land beyond the Tamar. England was now, to all intents and purposes, Saxon.

The newcomers soon imposed their own patterns on the land. It had been won in battle and the victors were, not surprisingly, conscious of the need for defence. So a basic unit was devised—the burh. It seems to have been developed around the time of Alfred the Great. In effect, the burhs were forts so arranged that no one in the kingdom was more than twenty-five miles from the safety of one of them. Each of these burhs had land around it, parcelled out into hides, an area that could be anything from sixty to a hundred acres, and each hide had to supply one man for the defences. There was a very strict correlation between the number of hides and the size of the burh, the intention being to ensure that men could be posted at roughly five-foot intervals all around the walls. One might expect many of the burhs to be based on the existing fortified towns left by the Romans, but many of these were already in ruins. This description by a Saxon poet is generally taken to refer to Bath.

> Wonderful is this wall of stone, wrecked by fate
> The city buildings crumble, the bold works of the giants decay.
> Roofs have caved in, towers collapsed,
> Barred gates are gone, gateways have gaping mouths,
> Hoar frost clings to mortar.
>
> (*trans*. K. Crossley-Holland)

Where the old fortifications still stood, as at Colchester for example, then the Saxons made use of them. Elsewhere they began their own settlements, using much the same criteria for siting them as the Romans had done—strategic importance and defensibility. Inevitably a high proportion were built up beside rivers. The town of Wallingford on the Thames is an excellent example of a Saxon burh.

The name at once suggests that this was a fording place before the town was begun, and the name is probably a corruption from the 'ford of Wealh's people', or the ford of the Welsh. It is quite possible that like much of the Thames valley, the site was occupied long before the Saxon period, and there have been finds suggesting bronze age and iron age occupation. The Romans, however, showed no interest whatsoever in the place and their main road from Silchester to Dorchester passed by to the east. The earliest definite reference to the new settlement comes in a ninth-century land deed which refers to Waelingford.

As a fording place on the river, the site had an obvious strategic importance, while the river itself helped to make the site defensible. Details of the burh with its attached lands parcelled out into hides are given in a great document dating from the early tenth century, the Burghal Hideage. This gives Wallingford 2,400 hides, which would correspond to a defensive wall of 3,016 metres, assuming that the planners followed the rules of one man per hide spaced out round the wall. The wall itself can be seen today as a high bank which encloses the town on three sides, the fourth side being bounded by the Thames. Yet, if you measure the bank you find that it is 274 metres short of the proper measurement to correspond with the Burghal Hideage. Had the planners got their sums wrong? Across the river is a ditch, which corresponds to the modern borough boundary. It would seem reasonable to suppose that the Saxons wanted to have a defensive position across the river to control the bridgehead. Add the length of the ditch to the town bank and this time the figures come out just right.

Wallingford was only one of many burhs established along the rivers of Saxon England. Many flourished, as did some of the older centres. London remained a busy port, described by Bede as 'the exchange port of many nations'. A Saxon wharf has been excavated at New Fresh Wharf, between London Bridge and Billingsgate. The Thames itself was a major trading route, at least as far upstream as Abingdon, though just how easy it was to get a boat up the river is by no means clear. Since however the authorities were prepared to spend money on river improvement, there must have been a reasonable volume of trade. Navigation was important, but there were others besides boatmen looking to spend their lives by the rivers.

Christianity came to Britain in Saxon times, and the early Christian missionaries brought with them more than just religious precepts. Bede credits Bishop Wilfred with saving Sussex from starvation in the seventh century by teaching the locals how to fish, 'for their seas and rivers abounded in fish, but the people had no skill to take them, except eels alone'. It seems unlikely that the locals were quite as inept as Bede suggests, but certainly fishing became important, since fish was part of the religious diet. By the end of the tenth century, the fishing industry was well established. In the *Colloquies of Aelfric*, written around 990, various tradesmen describe their work, fishermen amongst them: 'I go on board my boat and cast my net into the river, and cast my angle and baits, and what they catch I take. I cast the unclean fish away and take the clean for meat. The citizens buy my fish, I cannot catch as many as I can sell. Eel and pike, minnows and eel-pout, trout and lampreys.'

Others might go out on the high seas in search of far bigger game, but our river fisherman has no ambitions in that direction: 'It is a perilous thing to catch a whale. It is pleasanter for me to go to the river with my boat than to go with many boats whale hunting.' (*Trans*. B. Thorpe)

Fishing was circumscribed by many rules and regulations. The fisherman quoted above drew a distinction between 'clean' and 'unclean' fish—a distinction dictated by the church on doctrinal rather than hygienic grounds in rules first recorded by Archbishop Ecghbert (735–66). There was also the difficult question of who owned the fish. On many rivers, fish traps known as basket weirs or simply weirs were set. A survey of an estate at Tidenham in Gloucestershire recorded 30 basket weirs on the Severn at Stroat, 21 at Kingston, where there were a further 12 on the Wye, 15 on the Wye at Bishton and 9 at Landcaut. The whole estate consisted of 30 hides, of which 21 hides were occupied by tenants, who were by no means allowed to keep all that they caught. 'At every weir within the 30 hides every alternate fish belongs to the lord of the manor, and every rare fish which is of value—sturgeon or porpoise, herring or sea fish—and no one has the right of selling any fish for money when the lord is on the estate without informing him about it.'

The use of the word 'weir' can be confusing, as it was also used in the modern sense of a barrier across the river, built to control the flow of water. Many weirs of this type were constructed to ensure a regular supply of water for the mills, a subject we shall be looking at later. These weirs were also used by fishermen to set their traps. The peaceful use of rivers was everywhere increasing—but those same rivers were about to be used for less peaceful purposes.

By the eighth century, overseas trade was a commonplace, and was controlled by officials to whom all traders were supposed to report, a kind of Saxon Customs Officer. One day in 789, an unfamiliar vessel was reported to have landed on the English shore and a burh official no doubt, possibly grumbling at the inconvenience, went down to collect the humdrum details of the journey. He approached the visitors, but if there was any exchange of information it did not last long. The newcomers drew their swords and killed the official: the first Vikings had arrived. For the next two centuries and more, they were to make repeated forays into Britain. Sometimes they would be brief forays for booty, at other times they would be longer campaigns ending in settlement. But the first notable acts were acts of destruction recorded by the chroniclers on 8 January 793 when 'the heathen men lamentably destroyed God's church at Lindisfarne'. The early attacks took the raiders across the North Sea and up the Northumbrian coast to Scotland and the rich pickings in the Celtic monasteries and churches of the east coast. They were a warrior race from Scandinavia and they possessed one great advantage—they had better ships and better seamen than any other European power.

The Viking longship was a major advance on the Saxon vessels of the Sutton Hoo type. The latter had very little keel and were longitudinally very weak, which meant that they were liable to break their backs in high seas. So sea voyages were kept as short as possible. They ran along the coast to the shortest crossing point then scuttled across the Channel to the opposite shore. The long ship was a real sea-going vessel. As with the Sutton Hoo ship, we owe most of our knowledge of these fine vessels to burial ships, unearthed by archaeologists. The grandest Viking ship was found at Gokstad in Norway in a burial mound believed to be that of King Olaf Geirsted-Alv, who died around 800.

The Gokstad ship is 78 foot long, 17 foot beam and 6¾ foot deep, with steeply raked bows and stern and a prominent keel. The sides are built up higher than in the Saxon boats and have rowing ports cut into them. There were sixteen oars on each side, and a single mast was set amidships. With their ferocious figureheads and equally ferocious crew, they must have brought terror to the British as they loomed up out of the North Sea. The terror is a thousand years behind us, and today we can admire the sheer beauty of such craft, a beauty which derives, as in all the great ships, from the lines of the hull. It is a beauty born from a practical design problem, the need to devise a vessel which could cope with the heavy seas around Scandinavia, yet which had to be shallow and narrow enough to make use of navigable rivers. They were vessels which would be used for trade or its criminal counterpart, piracy, but above all else they had to be raiding vessels. They performed all tasks admirably, though it is doubtful whether many of the local inhabitants in those early days took time off to admire these sleek thoroughbreds of the northern ocean.

The first Viking raiders stayed close to the coast, but in time they moved ever further up the rivers. Their raids were daring in plan and execution. In 1009, for example, Olaf the Stout brought his fleet up the Thames towards London Bridge. Defenders lined up along the bridge were armed with an impressive array of missiles of all sorts from stones to spears. They seemed to be an effective barrier to any further progress, but Olaf managed to get part of his force right in underneath the bridge. They used improvised hurdles to protect themselves from the stones and the men held their shields over their heads, though the greatest danger was not of individual injury but of a boat being holed. Under this cover, Olaf's men fastened ropes to the piers of the bridge and rowed as hard as they could downstream. The piers were no more than wooden posts, which were soon pulled down. The bridge collapsed, throwing the defenders into the Thames and the way through London was open.

The Vikings were more than just hit-and-run raiders. They were conquerors, demanding and receiving tribute. When King Swein of Denmark brought his force to Britain in 1013, he took his fleet right up the Humber and the Trent to Gainsborough. There was no need for battle: the locals submitted without a fight, handing over hostages and leaving Swein free to march south. It was only one of a series of such campaigns in which the Norsemen and the Saxons fought for the control of Britain. Where the Norsemen established their control, they were able to settle down to a more peaceful way of life, working as craftsmen, traders and farmers. They were even able to establish their own provincial capital at York, a natural centre for their purposes, set well inland but with river access to the North Sea. Yet the periods of peace never seemed to last long, and even York was retaken by the Saxons.

The last major campaign was to have a decisive effect on the history of the country. King Hardrada of Norway laid claim to the English throne, then occupied by Harold. He ravaged the coast southwards from the Tyne with the help of Harold's own brother, Tastig. Their combined forces then sailed up the Humber. York surrendered and the invaders eventually made camp at Stamford Bridge to take a rest which, if not well earned, was certainly much needed. Harold, however, was already marching his army with incredible speed up from London. The Danes were totally unprepared when Harold's men stormed the camp. It was a great victory for the Saxons—and a great slaughter, commemorated right into modern times with a feast at which 'spear pies', pies baked in a boat-shaped crust, are eaten. The few Viking survivors took their ships back up the Humber. Their last attempt to rule Britain had ended.

It is usual to think of the Vikings as a purely destructive force, and in many ways that description could be justified. Monastic life in eastern and northern Britain was altogether shattered by the Norsemen, though they themselves were later to prove ready converts to Christianity. When captured, they were eager to abandon their old, evil, heathen ways and accept baptism: many were to be baptised in similar circumstances over and over again. Yet the Norsemen who stayed as settlers added a great deal to the life of the country. They brought with them new skills many of which were, not surprisingly, concerned with ships and the sea. They also brought their own ideas about the use of water power. No Roman water wheels survive in Britain, but wheels built to the Norse pattern do.

The Norse mill is the simplest form of water-powered mill. A vertical shaft with a horizontal wheel at the end is lowered into a fast-moving river or stream and the other end of the shaft carries the mill stone. As the wheel turns in the stream it drives the stone directly, without the need for any intermediate gearing. Such mills were common in the areas settled by the Vikings and the design survived for centuries. Just such a mill can be seen at Dounby in Orkney.

The Dounby mill is a useful reminder that some at least of the Vikings lived in peace, but it added little new, since it was inferior to the Roman Vitruvian water wheel. The Viking at war remains the dominant image from the period, the helmeted figure with axe and sword, and it was the Viking at war that brought this whole period of history to an end. After his defeat of Hardrada, Harold was forced to march his troops all the way south again to face a new threat. It was an exhausting journey which did nothing to prepare the troops for the battle that was still to come. They had beaten the Norsemen, and now they, in turn, were defeated by the men led by William of Normandy. It could be argued that the Battle of Hastings in 1066 was decided at the Battle of Stamford Bridge. The age of Anglo-Saxon rule was over. Norman rule had begun.

CHAPTER THREE

Chaucer's company

Those who search for portraits of the characters who made up medieval society must eventually find themselves sitting down with and taking delight in the company of Geoffrey Chaucer. The pilgrims assembled at the Tabard Inn in Southwark contained representatives of every order of society, all making their way to Canterbury. At the head of the company was the aristocracy, in the person of the knight with his entourage of squire and yeoman. After the aristocracy came the church in full measure—prioress, monk, friar, priest and parson, pardoner and summoner. The 'middle class' was represented by lawyers, merchants and the lesser landowners and, bringing up the rear as it were, were a group of tradesmen, such as the barge skipper, miller and ploughman. This may seem a slightly odd group to introduce at the beginning of a chapter which is supposed to be concerned with the relationship between man and rivers in medieval Britain, yet each of these groups would have found, to a quite remarkable extent, that rivers had affected their way of life.

Chaucer's first category, the aristocracy, might seem to be the least affected by such mundane matters as simple geography. Yet the first Norman lords were lords of conquest, and those who take the land by force are always most aware that they could lose it again in precisely the same way. The Saxons had fortified their new settlements, and the Normans followed their example. In the first years after the Conquest, William ruthlessly pushed ahead with the building of a new society, in which the land was to be controlled through powerful lords, each secure within his own castle and controlling his own well-armed troops. The beaten Saxons were pressed into service to construct motte and bailey castles. These consisted of a high earth mound, the motte, topped by a wooden tower, below which was the yard or bailey. This contained stone houses, barns and the homes of servants and troops, all surrounded by a deep ditch. Sometimes there were two ditches, filled with water, but it was still a makeshift expedient, and within a few years more solid defences were begun.

Fortresses needed to look to two possible sources of attack: those from overseas and those from within the British mainland. Norman England had two internal frontiers, with Wales and Scotland, both of which called for protection and it was on the Welsh border in particular that some of the finest Norman strongholds were constructed. After the Conquest, William granted the manor of Stanton, in what is now Shropshire, to one of his principal supporters, William de Lacy, a grant commemorated in the name of the village, Stanton Lacy. In return, de Lacy was required to keep guard over that section of the border, and he looked around for a suitable defensible position. He found what he wanted at a spot known by the Anglo-Saxon name of Ludlow, 'the hill by the loud waters'. The hill stood at the junction of the Teme and its tributary, the Corve, and on three sides it dropped down in steep cliffs to the water. It was here that Walter's son Roger de Lacy built Ludlow Castle at the end of the eleventh century. The pattern of the castle was still based on the motte and bailey, with a double moat hacked out of the hard rock. To this protection was added the strength of stone buildings and stone walls. It changed much over the years, and today only the curious circular chapel remains of the original Norman buildings. The original gatehouse was enlarged to form the keep, and, in the fifteenth century, when the castle was taken over by the Mortimers, the splendid great hall was added.

The need for fortification was proved more than once, though internal rivalries proved more of a threat than the Welsh. In 1139, Henry I's daughter, Matilda, was contending for the throne with her cousin Stephen. She found herself besieged behind the strong walls of Ludlow Castle. It was a long siege, during which the castle withstood many attacks, though the fortunes of the rival factions were almost transformed in one bizarre incident. Stephen was walking round the walls with an ally, Prince Henry of Scotland, when he suddenly found himself being hauled up into the air. A defender had gone fishing with a grappling hook at the end of a rope and had caught himself a king. Prince Henry drew his sword, cut the rope and Stephen descended to earth.

Ludlow is just one of a string of castles along the Welsh border, many of which took advantage of the river as a natural defence. Perhaps the most spectacular is Goodrich Castle, perched high on a crag above the Wye. Here the river forms the natural boundary between the two countries, and this great castle, begun in the twelfth century, had only one purpose—to guard the crossing. There could scarcely be a greater contrast between these two examples of Norman architecture when one looks at them today. At Ludlow, the castle forms the focus of the town that grew up under the protection of the lords, de Lacy and Mortimer: Goodrich remains isolated and aloof, the solitary fortress.

The Scottish border presented a quite different problem. Here again the river helped to define the limits and the important crossing point of the Tweed at Berwick was fortified. At the opposite end of the border, the old Roman fort by the Eden at Carlisle was taken over by William II in 1092. It had been claimed by the Scots, but William was having none of that and handed the fort over to a Norman lord, known as William the Priest, with orders to build a new castle and a church. Matters did not rest there. Carlisle was handed back to the Scots by Stephen, in exchange for a promise to stop giving aid to Matilda. Then it was taken back by the English in 1157. So, the pendulum swung over the castle by the Eden.

The conjunction of castle and river was almost inevitable on the borders where the river so often marked the boundary and the need to control crossing points was of paramount importance. The same conjunction also occurred throughout the countryside. The river crossings had the same importance in the constant skirmishes between rival factions inside the country as they had in international affairs. This was especially true of navigable rivers, where there was the added need to control traffic on the river as well as over it. So the greatest Norman fortress in England was built beside the country's most important river crossing, King William's own castle in London. Here he established his capital, and the first hastily built motte and bailey was soon replaced by the great White Tower. Built around 1080, the building rises ninety feet above the banks of the Thames.

The castle standing above the river has become the very emblem of the feudal lord. From the top of his tower he could look down on the rest of the world. The only buildings that could rival the castle for size and splendour were those of the church, the great abbeys and monasteries that were home to Chaucer's second group of pilgrims. Chaucer's knight, recently returned from the crusades, is given his full measure of praise:

> A knight there was, and that a worthy man,
> That from the time that he first began
> To riden out, he loved chivalry,
> Truth and honour, freedom and courtesy.

On the other hand, the poet had scarcely a decent word to say for any of his assortment of nuns, priests and friars. They were often quite wealthy. The Nun Prioress, for example, wore brightly coloured beads and bracelets, and

> a golden brooch of brightest sheen,
> On which there first was graven a crowned A,
> And lower *Amor vincit omnia.*

Not perhaps the most apt sentiment for a lady who had taken the vow of chastity. The monk, given to hunting and high living, is joined by the friar who knew that the true price of penitence could be measured in the penitents' coin:

> For many a man so hard is of heart
> He may not weep, although he sorely smart,
> Therefore, instead of weeping and prayers,
> Man must give silver to the poor friars.

His most damning condemnation of the clergy is put into the mouth of another man, the summoner, who describes a friar's visit to hell in the company of an angel. The visitor is quite delighted not to see a single friar in the place. The angel quickly disillusions him, and turns to the devil.

> 'Hold up thy tail, thou Satanas!' quoth he,
> 'Show forth thy arse and let the friar see
> Where is the nest of friars in this place.'

Yet the great religious houses were begun by idealists who set the highest possible moral standards. The earliest order of monks in Britain were the Augustinians, who founded their rules on those laid down by St Benedict. The rules are very firm on a number of points. 'The sin of personal possession,' they declare, 'above all others, should be cut out by its roots from the monastery.' The main object of the monastery was to provide a place where the monks could praise God and there were to be seven offices each day, starting with matins and ending with compline, as well as a night office. On top of this, the brothers were expected to work, for 'idleness is the enemy of the soul'. Chaucer's monks received gifts from the wealthy. St Benedict's were only required to entertain all guests who came to the monastery, but not to mix with them. The life of the monastery was to be strict, and the vows of poverty, chastity and obedience to be taken seriously. Nothing should be done that would distract the brothers from their main purpose, the worship of God. All this is far removed from the venalities of Chaucer's pilgrims, yet the founders of the first monasteries did their best to ensure that the distractions of the world were minimized.

Water mills, drawn in 1814 at Llanfair, North Wales, by the celebrated water-colourist, David Cox.

A view of the Thames below Westminster Pier by Wenceslaus Hollar, about 1640.

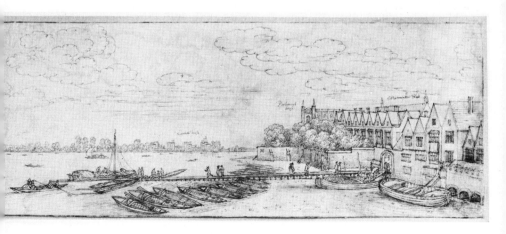

CHEALSEA REACH

Pleasure boating on Chelsea Reach, a river outing complete with musicians in 1799, by Rowlandson.

A busy river scene in Norwich in the early nineteenth century.

Liverpool docks at the beginning of the nineteenth century.

The castellated viaduct across the River Nidd at Knaresborough
makes a picturesque addition to a picturesque scene.

Punt fishing near London, mid-nineteenth century.

Eel anglers, 1834.

The ultimate irony of the change that came to the monasteries can be seen in the present day, when the once secluded sites are thronged by tourists, come to stare at the magnificent ruins of Tintern, Fountains or Bolton Abbey. It is an irony, because seclusion and inaccessibility were the lures which brought the builders to such spots in the first place. These spots were untamed. Beauty, and its companion distractions and temptations, lay in the towns: here was only wilderness. Fountains Abbey in Yorkshire occupied an ideal position, and its story is typical of many others.

St Mary's Abbey had been established in York, but in 1132, thirteen monks, feeling that life in the city was becoming soft and corrupt, decided to break away and establish their own foundation. They went to a deep, wooded valley of the River Skell. It was described by Archbishop Thurston of York as 'a place remote and uninhabited, set with thorns, amongst the hollows of the mountains and rocks, more fit, it seemed, for the lair of wild beasts than for human use'. It was, as a letter writer put it, 'a place of horror and vast solitude'.

The first monks lived in a thatched hut, and at times were reduced to cooking leaves from the trees for food. The river was their chief source of life: it gave them water to drink and fish to eat. It was an essential part of the life of the abbey, even after the monks had raised walls and put a roof over their head. The strict dietary rules of the church made fish an important part of their food supply, and as the remote spot chosen for the abbey gave the monks no opportunity for trade, they had to be self-sufficient. So, beside the quiet waters of the Skell, the quiet life of the abbey continued. But the days of extreme hardship faced by the founders were short lived. In 1135, Hugh, the Dean of York, decided to retire to Fountains Abbey, but not to a life of unremitting austerity. He brought with him his extensive library for study and extensive funds for building. Other endowments followed from the local aristocracy, and the abbey grew and developed, until by the end of the thirteenth century it was the richest Cistercian house in all England.

The new abbey had magnificent architecture and a thriving community, including as many as 600 lay brothers who, not having sufficient scholarship for the priesthood, were given the task of farming the abbey estates. The religious order, which disavowed all personal property, wrangled interminably with neighbours over land ownership. They covered the surrounding countryside with new stone walls to establish their property, and they used huge tracts of land to graze their flocks of as many as 15,000 head of sheep. The Skell could no longer supply the fish to feed this new multitude, so its waters were diverted to fill artificial fish ponds, where fish could be farmed. In all, these ponds covered twenty acres of abbey land.

The transformation of the monastic foundations from communities of the abstemious poor to centres of wealth and rich living had profound effects on the country. The monasteries and abbeys were great landowners and attitudes towards the land inevitably changed. The first monks hunting out the remote valleys were looking for wilderness; the new generation saw the land as a usable asset. The rivers were now farmed as the land was farmed, and were put to use. Navigation was improved at the abbey's expense—with the abbey, of course, claiming the profits. There was a good deal of activity in the fens, where the monastic houses were responsible for programmes of land drainage, altering the rivers of the region and leaving vast areas that had once been marshland as grassland for sheep.

Abbey and abbot fattened up together. St Cuthbert in his retreat to the Farne Islands took the greatest delight in watching the wild animals and birds. When he was commemorated in the Neville screen at Durham, the device carved was that of the eider duck. Chaucer's monk also watched the wild birds that drifted past on the river, but from a rather different point of view: 'he liked a swan best, and roasted whole'. But if the abbot was venal, the abbeys remain among the finest monuments that the country possesses. Whether the founders were totally immune to what we now see as beautiful scenery is something that we cannot know, but that they had an eye for beauty no one can doubt. The buildings proclaim it. The discovery of beauty in the wild countryside that surrounded the abbeys—the moorland of Wharfedale at Bolton or the thick-wooded valley of the Wye at Tintern—is generally attributed to the picturesque movement of the eighteenth century. Medieval man was too preoccupied with lowering his eyes to the ground he worked for his livelihood or in the case of the priests and monks raising them to the sky, to have much time for contemplating the beauties of nature. Yet it is hard for anyone who has walked along the banks of the Wye on a summer's day not to believe that the pious monk—and even in later days there was still piety—did not take back to his cell some memory of light dancing on water. Perhaps he also shared something of the sensation that Wordsworth felt when he looked back on the day when he sat on the hillside above Tintern:

> But oft, in lonely rooms, and 'mid the din
> Of towns and cities, I have owed to them,
> In hours of weariness, sensations sweet,
> Felt in the blood, and felt along the heart;

And passing even into my purer mind
With tranquil restoration.

Knight and priest made their homes on the river banks, though for rather different reasons. Some abbeys and some castles remained isolated in the wild, while others formed the nuclei around which towns developed. Ludlow is one example of a market town which developed in the shelter of the castle walls. There is an even more striking example of the castle-borough in Wales at Pembroke. The castle was built at the riverside and was approached by a straight road that ran along a ridge parallel to the river. In the early twelfth century, Gilbert de Clare laid out a town based on tenements on either side of the approach road, and enclosed the whole within a defensive wall. Powerful abbots were no less enthusiastic town founders. The abbey at Eynsham stood beside the Chit Brook, a little tributary of the Thames. The abbey prospered and King Stephen granted it a market about 1135, and a market place was established to the north of the abbey. Houses were built around the new market and along the main street from the abbey. Continuing prosperity encouraged later abbots to increase the size of the town, and in 1215 another area was laid out for housing, known as Newland, and still reached by Newland Street. Such examples could be repeated many times over, as the riverside sites developed into riverside towns, even though the original importance of the river was later lost.

These were not the only founders of new towns. Three kings in particular, Richard I, John and Henry III, were great providers of royal charters, which gave the towns considerable freedom to regulate their own affairs. In return, the towns provided much-needed cash for the three monarchs. Liverpool, for example, owes its foundation to John, who in letters patent of 1207 invited 'his faithful people' to settle there. The town was given its official charter in 1229 by Henry III. It contained a clause which presaged the town's later role as one of the country's most important ports.

> We have granted to the said burgesses and their heirs that any merchant bound for the said borough with their wares, from whatever place they come, whether they are foreigners or others, dwellers within our peace, or have come to our country by our licence, shall be brought safe and sound to the said borough with their wares, and shall stay there in safety, and in safety shall return, paying the proper and due customs on their trade.

The Black Death put an end to the foundation of new towns, but in the earlier period of prosperity the towns thrived and grew. Trade grew with the prosperity, but trade requires transport and, as always, the rivers were both a help and a hindrance. Cargo boats used the few navigable waterways, while all rivers formed a barrier to road traffic which had to cross by ford, ferry or bridge. Chaucer's next group knew all about rivers. The merchants used them and contributed to the cost of bridging them: the lawyers were kept well supplied with fees, as they sorted out the rival claims of the transport users.

The quantity and quality of medieval bridges can be guessed at from the surprisingly large number of survivors, though it is not always easy to guess at the nature of the roads themselves and the traffic they carried. There were pack-horse routes along which strings of horses were led, each fully loaded with merchandise, and many of these routes survive as bridle paths and tracks. Then there were the abbey roads, linking the abbey to the granges and farms or, in the case of the wealthier foundations, to the markets and ports. Such a trade could be considerable. In the early fourteenth century, Fountains Abbey had a wool crop of more than twelve tons a year, much of which went to the port of Boston on the Witham in Lincolnshire. Drove roads crossed the country, wide trackways used by cattle, sheep, geese, pigs, any animal that needed to be driven long distances to market. On the whole, these passed through relatively empty countryside, where the stopping places are still commemorated by lonely pubs with names such as the Drovers Arms. These roads avoided the problems of river crossings by keeping as far as possible to the uplands, where the rivers were narrow, shallow and easily forded. Highland cattle coming down the western side of Scotland had a regular ford across the Solway to the west of Carlisle. Then there were the major highways, some of which followed the old Roman roads. It was a busy scene on the roads—strings of pack-horses, lumbering ox wagons, droves of animals and an assortment of travellers, merchants and pilgrims, beggars and thieves.

Drove roads present few problems, since the busy traffic makes its own road by regular use, trampling out a wide roadway. Such routes, in fact, continued in use until modern times and the sight of huge herds and flocks moving around the country was a commonplace even in the days of railways. The drovers brought their animals over long distances, and the beasts had to be shod for the journey. Cattle were shod like horses with iron shoes, while pigs had special boots made for them and the geese had their feet hardened with tar. Because they avoided the rivers, they left few signs of their passage in that quarter, apart from the many 'ford' endings to names of riverside villages and towns.

The pack-horse routes formed a much more extensive and complex network, joining towns and villages all over the country. It was quite impossible for these routes to avoid river crossings, and pack-horse bridges developed their own distinctive characteristics. Because the horses' packs were generally in the form of panniers slung on either side of the animal, the ideal bridge was narrow, to save on the cost of construction, and either had no parapet at all, or else a very low one, which the panniers could clear. Many examples have survived, especially in the north of England. There is an excellent example over Oak Beck near Harrogate in Yorkshire. It could scarcely be simpler, a rough stone arch in the shape of a segment of a circle, roughly built and with no parapet. The pack-horse bridge could be somewhat grander, and one of the finest can be seen at the opposite end of the country, a thirteenth-century bridge with three arches at Coombe Bissett, near Salisbury. But all these bridges have one thing in common—plainness. They were built for trade and used almost exclusively by traders, and while there is money in trade, there is no percentage in decoration. So simplicity not elaboration was the order. The semi-circular or segmented arch was taken over from the Romans and became the norm. Not that simplicity and plainness should imply ugliness—far from it. The stonework has mellowed and coloured with time, and the little bridge at the end of a sunken, twisting road is a poignant reminder of a vanished past.

When, however, it came to building a town bridge, quite different matters had to be considered. The bridge was expected to reflect the dignity and importance of the city or town, though there was often more enthusiasm over its design and construction than there was over its maintenance once it had been completed. Bridges, like roads, had to be maintained by the compulsory labour of the local citizens. It is all very well passing laws dictating how many days' work the citizen should do—less easy to specify how much work he should do on those days, or how well he should do it. Some treated the work days as holidays, others paid labourers to take their place. A disorganized, unskilled and largely unwilling labour force is not likely to make the best of a job, and so it proved in practice. The River Tyne, for example, was first bridged at Corbridge in 1235, when permission was given to place one end of the bridge on Lord Dilston's land. Seventy years later, however, the bridge was in a sorry, not to say lethal, condition. The Patent Rolls for 1304 recorded that a commission had been appointed 'touching default of the repair of the bridge at Corbridge, Northumberland which is so broken down that men wishing to cross it have been drowned . . . alms collected for its repair are said to have been converted to their profit in carrying on trade'. Protection of bridges was, in fact, needed long after this time. The twelfth-century White Mill Bridge at Sturminster Marshall in Dorset has a notice, dating from the reign of George IV announcing that 'any person willfully injuring any part of this County Bridge will be guilty of felony and upon conviction liable to be transported for life'. The Corbridge Bridge never lasted that long. It was eventually replaced in 1674, and the new bridge was the only one across the Tyne to survive the great flood of 1771. Even then it was almost submerged, and the locals could lean over the parapet and dangle their fingers in the water. The other medieval bridges were less fortunate. Newcastle had already lost an early wooden bridge, which was destroyed by fire and replaced in 1248 by a stone bridge which, according to Leland, 'hath 10 Arches and a Stronge Warde and Tower on it'. Descriptions of this bridge disagree over the number of arches, which might seem a little strange, since one would assume that anyone sufficiently interested to write a description of the thing would at least have the gumption to count up to ten with reasonable accuracy. In fact, it is not really all that odd. Medieval bridges often had more arches set down on the land than they did over the water. The width of the arch was limited, and the small land arches were often converted into cellars and storerooms. After conversion, they were sometimes left out of the count. In the 1771 flood, the two central arches of this bridge were demolished by the waters which also carried away eight houses. One wooden house was carried nearly eight miles, and when it was found, a dog and a cat were discovered inside, both alive and well and apparently none the worse for the voyage. If details of the Newcastle bridge are a little vague, we do know that it had at least one of the characteristics of important medieval bridges. It was fortified.

The fortified bridge was an essential part of the fortified town, there not being a great deal of sense in going to all the trouble of building fortifications, if you are going to leave the bridge open to anyone who felt like marching an army across. Although such bridges were once quite common, few have survived. Once the need for defence had disappeared, the narrow fortified gateway just became a blockage on the road. One splendid example, however, can still be seen at Monmouth. The medieval town was entered through four gates, and the last of these gates stands on the bridge across the River Monnow. The bridge house had a portcullis which could be dropped to close the roadway.

The church played an important part in bridge building, quite often to meet their own needs, although the needs of others were also seen to at the same time. The Abbot's Bridge at Bury St Edmunds had a main roadway for horses and vehicles and plank walkways at the side: one side for laity, the other for monks. All this bridge building greatly eased the business of travelling, though moving around the country was still a slow and often dangerous affair. The prudent man looked for all the protection he could get, and he did not necessarily have to step far out of his way to get the blessing of the church. Bridges, such as that at St Ives in Cambridgeshire had their own chapels built into the fabric. Visitors to the St Ives chapel, in more recent times, might have called in for quite different types of blessing, and for advice on someone else's horse rather than their own mount, for the patron saint of the chapel was St Leger. The church also helped with some novel forms of fund raising. The Bishop of Worcester offered free indulgencies to all who contributed to the bridge over the Severn.

The medieval bridge came, not surprisingly, in a variety of shapes and sizes, depending on the job it was required to do. At Crowland in Lincolnshire there is an extraordinary triple bridge which once crossed three streams, now long since dried up. There were a number of very long, low bridges carried on many arches, such as the twenty-four-arched bridge at Bideford in Devon. The first bridge was built of wood in 1315, and converted to stone in the fifteenth century. In time, bridge builders came to use the pointed Gothic arch as well as the rounded Romanesque, and an example can be seen in what is perhaps the finest of all our medieval bridges, which crosses the little River Till, a tributary of the Tweed. Its date is unknown, but it was not new when John Leland went on his reporting tour of Britain in the 1530s. He described it as 'of Stone one bow, both greate and stronge'. So it is and, one could add, superbly elegant. It has a pointed arch, ninety foot in span with a rise of nearly forty foot. It is supported by five narrow, chamfered ribs. It is magnificent, though sadly it was modernized and given a new parapet by nineteenth-century 'improvers'.

Where there was no bridge or ford, there was often a ferry. The Severn, for example, had two ferries near Chepstow. One was still in use during the Civil War, when a Royalist boatman took a troop of Parliamentarians across and managed to persuade them that a mudbank they had reached was, in fact, the shore. They disembarked and there the boatmen left them to drown. There seems to have been little improvement in the service over the years—though fewer deliberate drownings. As late as the eighteenth

55

century, John Gilpin described the 'miserable walk to the boat through the sludge; and over shelving and slippery rocks . . . The boat after some struggling with the shelves, at length gained the channel. After beating almost near two hours against the wind our voyage concluded, as it began, with an uncomfortable walk through the sludge to high water mark.' The ferryman, if contemporary tales are anything to go by, would not have been unduly concerned at his passengers' discomfort. The *Hundred Merry Tales* of 1526—the only book that Shakespeare ever refers to by name in his plays, in *Much Ado About Nothing*—has a story about a ferryman. Two men were being taken across a river and during the journey they quarrelled, then fought and the affair ended with one being thrown overboard and drowning. This roused the ferryman to righteous anger: 'beshrew thy heart thou shouldest have taryed and foughte with him a lande, for now thou hast caused me to lose an halfpenny for my fare.'

The scale and quality of surviving medieval bridges—and survival is, by itself, one measure of the quality—indicate the rapid growth of internal traffic in the country. The roads were busy and traffic over the bridges was heavy and so, in some cases, was the traffic beneath them. Rivers, as well as roads, took their share of increasing trade. The Thames has always been considered the most important of Britain's rivers, if only because London is the major port. But the River Severn can boast a longer navigable length, and through its connection via the Avon it also gave access to what was for a long time the second port of the land, Bristol.

The Severn today is only navigable by large craft as far as Bewdley, though there is some hope of extending navigation as far as Bridgnorth, but in medieval times boats could reach as far north as Shrewsbury. There were two main types of vessel in use on the river: rafts, described by Leland as 'many flatt and long vessels to carry up and downe all manner of merchandise' and the Severn trows. The name 'trow' has, over the centuries, been used to describe a wide variety of craft, but generally refers to a sailing barge. The name 'barge', in turn, probably derives from the Latin 'barca', meaning ship's boat or lighter. The earliest barges were little more than flat-bottomed wooden boxes, with a central mast and a single square sail. Even the later, more sophisticated trows, with their complex sail patterns, still had many of the same characteristics. The shape of the hull became less square in time, and the traditional trow was noted for its D-shaped transom. It kept the flat bottom, which enabled the boat to be run aground on the tidal river, where it would stay upright for loading and unloading before floating off again at high tide. In general, the trows used below Gloucester were considerably larger than those used above, and separate boat-building centres developed. Bridgnorth was the great building centre for the upper river, Chepstow its equivalent for the lower reaches.

The problem with the simply rigged, square-sailed trow was that it could only take the wind on one side of the sail, so when changing course or tacking, the sail had to be turned round by hand. In the narrow confines of the river, the boat was pretty well limited to sailing only when there was a following wind. The rest of the time, the trow had to be bow-hauled, pulled along by gangs of men walking the towpath. These trowmen were specialists, working in gangs of about twenty. At Bewdley, they were traditionally signed up over a mug of ale at the Mug House on Coles Quay.

Numerous inland ports developed along the length of the river. Gloucester, Worcester, Bewdley and Bridgnorth were the four main centres, and there was intense rivalry between them. Gloucester was able to stand somewhat aloof from this bickering, since it marked the end of the line for larger vessels. The rest squabbled endlessly over the small boat trade. Worcester was the most important centre and generated a good deal of trade on its own account. Bewdley was built on the site of an ancient ford, where the trackway from Kidderminster to the Wyre Forest crossed the river. It was thus established at a point where road and river traffic met, and Bewdley became established as a major centre for the pack-horse trade. This reached a peak in the seventeenth century when as many as 400 animals were stabled in the town. Bridgnorth being near the limit of navigation had the advantage that it was the nearest port for all the traffic coming down from the north. It suffered, however, from the disadvantage that the river between there and Bewdley was notorious for its shallows and shoals. In dry spells, boats were often stranded for days waiting for a 'freshet', a sudden flash of water following rain in the Welsh hills where the Severn has its source. Each of the ports could lay claim to trade on its own merits, but they were seldom content with that. The Severn was an unimproved river, free to all users. That, at least, was the theory. In 1411, the burgesses of Bristol and Gloucester petitioned Parliament over Bewdley's attempt to monopolize trade by methods which were little short of piracy:

> Certain persons of Bewdley having great boats called trows have confederated themselves together for their singular profit and would let none pass through the said parts with their goods and chattels, except they would hire

the said boats for the carriage of the said goods: and on the eve of St Michael last past, lying in wait near Bewdley with great force and arms they had seized upon a great drag or flote going to Gloucester, and made the masters of it cut in pieces the said flote in the said river, or otherwise they would cut off their heads. They therefore pray free passage.

The authorities of Worcester joined the fray, claiming the right to charge a fee to all boats going under their bridge. This right was denied by an Act of Parliament of 1430, which avowed that 'the river Severn is common to all the King's liege people to carry and recarry all manner of merchandise as well in trowes and boats, as in flotes otherwise called drags'. Worcester got some compensation when, in 1504, they were given permission to make a charge on boats using the town quay. They put their own unique interpretation on the rule by assuming that this meant they were entitled to stop all passing traffic to ensure that they did use the quay. The Bewdley boatmen complained of being forced to 'cum out of the Kynge's hye streym' to pay the toll, and even being made to sell their goods then and there at a considerably lower price than they would have fetched in Gloucester or Bristol. Those boatmen who resisted were stoned by the good citizens from their vantage point on Worcester bridge. Chaucer's skipper of the barge *Maudelayne* would have felt quite at home on such a river where his own standards seemed to rule:

> And certainly he was a good fellow
> Full many a draught of wine had he drawn
> From Bordeaux, while that the trader sleep.
> Of nice conscience took he no keep.

The barge appeared in various guises on different rivers, and was transformed into something altogether grander than a simple trading vessel in 1454, when John Norman was chosen Mayor of London. He decided to make the journey to Westminster by water rather than by road and ordered an ornate and colourful barge to be built at his own expense. The City Companies, not wishing to be outdone by the new mayor, ordered equally grand barges of their own and the trip up the river was transformed into 'a most beautiful aquaous Triumph'. Where the mayor had led, royalty followed and surpassed, and the State Barge became the most opulent boat on the river. It was the sight of such craft on the Thames that inspired Shakespeare's description of Cleopatra's journey to her first meeting with Mark Antony:

> The barge she sat in, like a burnished throne,
> Burn'd on the water; the poop was beaten gold,

Purple the sails, and so perfumed that
The winds were love-sick with them; the oars were silver,
Which to the tune of flutes kept stroke, and made
The water which they beat to follow faster,
As amorous of their strokes.

The river that bore such splendid craft, even if they could never quite compete with Cleopatra's, also had humbler tasks to perform. If any one feature marked the rivers of medieval Britain as different from an earlier age, then it was the water wheel turning beside the grain mill. The Domesday Book records 5,246 mills, of which the overwhelming majority were water mills, though some would have been worked by animals: the windmill had yet to appear in Britain. The miller was one of the great, central figures of medieval life. Britain was a country dependent on agriculture, especially on corn. Bread was the great staple food of the people, and between the growers of crops and the bakers of loaves stood the miller.

The mill existed within the feudal system. The building belonged to the Lord of the Manor, who held it by what was known as 'stoke right'. All grain had to be brought to his mill, and a proportion of the whole was deducted by the miller as payment. The actual amount varied from mill to mill, but was generally around one-sixteenth. The Lord of the Manor was, of course, able to grind his own corn free of charge. It was, from the Lord's point of view, a very profitable system, though the tenants were not always equally enamoured of it. Some were tempted to grind their own corn at home using the rotary quern, a device consisting of a pair of small millstones, turned by hand. This was illegal and the Abbot of St Albans paved a courtyard with confiscated querns. The action was not forgotten, and during the Peasants' Revolt the whole courtyard was pulled up. In most places, the relationship between feudal lord and farmer was more equable. There was, however, still a good deal of distrust of the miller. The peasant brought so much grain to the mill and had no way of accurately assessing just how much flour he should receive. Chaucer's miller was certainly not scrupulous when collecting his toll:

A thief he was forsooth of corn and meal
And that a sly and usuant for to steal.

The dishonest miller got his well-earned comeuppance in the Reeve's Tale, and perhaps because it is one of the best known and most entertaining of the *Canterbury Tales*, its protagonist 'Simpkin the Swagger' has stood as the archetype of the medieval miller. We have no means of knowing how common such characters were in fact, but it would seem likely that if every miller was as dishonest as Simpkin there would have been something like a general uprising against the mills.

The miller led an isolated existence, for the mill was often set well away from the village. He was a hard-working man, running his mill single-handed, usually supplementing his income with eels from the river and perhaps keeping a few animals, fed on the grist left over from grinding. Water mills are still a fairly common sight along the rivers of Britain, even if very few still work. But those few which do are examples of an amazing continuity of use. Many an eighteenth- or nineteenth-century corn mill will be found to stand on a site mentioned in Domesday. Yet because of this very continuity, the medieval mill as such has vanished, replaced by more efficient successors. Looking at an eighteenth-century or later mill gives a false impression of what the early mills were like. These later mills were generally far larger than their medieval forerunners, and served a much wider community. Yet these later mills do show us one thing—they show us how the old mills worked.

During the medieval period, there were a great many improvements to the mill, especially to the power source, the water wheel. The earliest wheels were undershot, that is, the water met the blades at the lower part of the wheel, which stood directly in the flowing water of the river. As the rate of flow of the river was uncontrollable, so the speed of the wheel was uncontrollable. The mill builders, the millwrights, soon realized that if a weir was built across the river, part of the water could be diverted down an artificial channel to the mill. This water could be kept at a constant depth by means of movable sluices, and it could be directed to run just as the miller wished. Having control of his water supply, the millwright could then set about ways of building a better wheel. The undershot wheel is comparatively inefficient, but the millwright soon found that he could improve its performance by sinking it in a pit, so that the water hit the paddles halfway up the wheel. This type, known as the breastshot wheel, was a great improvement. He could go even further, by taking the water from a position higher upstream, and bringing it along in a wooden aqueduct or launder so that when it reached the mill, it was above the top of the wheel. The wheel itself was then fitted with a type of bucket instead of a straight paddle. The water could then drop into the buckets, and the weight would carry the wheel round. And that made a third, and very efficient, type of wheel, the overshot. An illustration in the fourteenth-century Luttrell Psalter shows a tiny mill with an overshot wheel, and the miller's eel traps can be seen in the stream.

Inside, the mill is a monument to the skill of the first professional engineers, the millwrights. At the very heart of the mill are the millstones which grind the corn. The lower stone, the bed stone, is set solidly in the mill floor and the upper stone, or runner, rotates above it. Each stone is cut with an intricate pattern of grooves, and the grooves cross each other, their edges acting like scissor blades to slice the grain. It is essential that the stones are properly balanced and kept in a horizontal plane, and this is where the true art of the millwright lies. The water wheel moves in a vertical plane and the millstones in a horizontal, and in between is the gearing which must keep the whole system in balance. As the water wheel turns, so a toothed wheel, known as the pit wheel, turns on the same axle. This connects with a horizontal gear wheel, the wallower, which rotates a vertical shaft on which a pair of stones can be set. In a larger mill, subsidiary gearing can be used to turn two or more pairs of stones.

Such a simple description disguises the complexity of the mill work. The gearing itself was vastly improved over the years, from the old-style lantern pinion, a device in which pegs on the rim of the pit wheel connected with another set of pegs, held between two wooden discs, forming the wallower. Later versions used the familiar cog wheels, exactly the same in principle as those used in all kinds of modern machinery. In fact much of our modern machinery has developed out of the craft of the millwright, but where the modern engineer has mass-produced metal components to deal with, his medieval forebear had to make each element as a one-off job, using wood instead of iron or steel. There was no standardization for him, and using wood presented its own special problems. Timber changes with age, and the process of ageing and seasoning had to be taken into account in the design. The millwright was an ingenious man, whose work greatly eased the labours of the miller. The actual process of grinding involves grain starting at the top of the mill, then falling under gravity through the stones to the bottom—but first it has to be raised up to the top to start its downhill journey. The millwright soon solved that little problem, introducing the simple sack hoist, worked by the turning shaft. No millwrights' names feature in the medieval rolls of honour, but if skill and imagination deserve to be recognized, then they deserve recognition.

The miller himself was a man who worked from practical experience,

61

rather than from any book of rules. He controlled the rate of flow of the grain, the fineness of the flour. If high-quality, fine flour was needed, it was sifted through a double sieve, known as a temse. As the two parts rubbed against each other they were warmed by friction, and the less vigorous sifter was informed that he would 'never set the temse on fire'.

The siting of a mill was at least as important as its detailed mechanism. The grinding of the stockpiles of corn was so vital to survival, that a mill was frequently included within a town's defences. At Southampton, there was a water wheel at the foot of God's House Tower, part of the defensive system. Elsewhere, it was a question of suitable water supply rather than defence which decided the issue of where the mill was to be placed. Tidal rivers, with their high rise and fall, provided special problems and were largely avoided, though a few mills were built specifically to use the tide. In the tide mill, the water rising up the creeks and estuaries is held back in mill ponds and then released to turn the wheel. Although they were not very common, a number have survived, including fine examples at Beaulieu in Hampshire, Woodbridge in Suffolk, at Carew Castle in Dyfed, and even in the heart of London, where a tidal mill straddles Bow Creek. These, however, were the exceptions, and the great majority of mills were spread around the countryside, and there is scarcely a river throughout Britain which has not, at some time or other, been pressed into service to work a grain mill. Unfortunately, the miller's idea of the best way to use a river did not always coincide with the ideas of those who wanted to use it for trade. His weirs blocked navigation and the water he drew off for his mill pond could leave the river dangerously short of water for boats. That problem was to increase enormously as navigation and water-wheel usage expanded simultaneously.

Chaucer's list of pilgrims covered most but by no means all of the river users. The river is a generous provider, and man found many uses for the riverside plants. Rushes were collected for strewing on the floor as a primitive carpet, for dipping in tallow to make rush lights and for thatching. Perhaps the most useful of all riverside plants was the willow. It was used for making everything from baskets to coracles, and in a variety of industries, such as tanning. Baskets were made from a special type of willow known as the osier, and osier cultivation continued right down to modern times.

H. R. Robinson in his book, *Life on the Upper Thames*, published in 1875, gives a very full description of osier harvesting as it was in his day, and it seems to have changed very little over the centuries. The osiers themselves were grown in clumps, often on islands, known on the Thames as 'holts' or 'hans'. They are very quick-growing plants, and after only a year's growth they can be anything from ten to fifteen foot high and ready for harvesting in the spring. 'Osier cutting is the hardest work—stooping from morning until night, and bending down the tall-headed willows with one hand, whilst the other wields the ponderous and sharp-edged hook.'

The osiers, known as 'rods', were then sorted by size, each size having its own traditional name—Luke, Threepenny, Middleborough and Great. The rods to be used for white baskets had to be peeled of their bark, and even as late as the 1870s the work was recorded by tallies. The rods were tied together in bundles of around forty-inch circumference, known as 'bolts', and when each bolt was completed it was taken to the overseer. He had two sticks for each stripper. When a bolt was completed, he put the two sticks together and made a cut across them both. He kept one stick and gave the other to the stripper. At the end of the day, the notches on each stick should tally exactly, so there was no chance of cheating by either side.

The river served man well, not least in providing him with fish in quantities and varieties that would astonish a modern angler. Some species which were commonplace, such as the delicious crayfish, have almost disappeared, while others, such as salmon and sea trout, have become luxuries. Overeagerness among fishermen, however, caused a great deal of anxiety, with the taking of young fish endangering the future stocks. Concern with conservation is not, it seems, a particularly modern preoccupation after all. As early as Edward I's reign there was a law prohibiting salmon fishing between the Nativity of Our Lady (8 September) and St Martin's Day (11 November). There was also a ban on fishing for young salmon which 'shall not be taken by nets, or by any other engine, at Millponds, from the midst of April into the Nativity of St John'. Those who broke the law had their nets confiscated and all their equipment destroyed: a second offence meant three months in gaol, a third offence a year and so on with ever-increasing sentences. It was still not enough to protect the fish, and an Act of 1389 banned the use of 'stalkers', very fine-meshed nets 'by which the fry or the breed of the salmons, lampreys or any other fish may in any wise be taken or destroyed'. Yet even then the problem was far from solved. In fact things had become so bad by the reign of Elizabeth I that a much more wide-ranging Act had to be introduced, and the preamble spelt out in detail just why it was necessary:

> The spawn, fry, and young breed of eels, salmon, pikes and all other fish, heretofore, hath been much destroyed in rivers and streams, salt and fresh

63

within this realm, insomuch that they feed swine and dogs with the fry and spawn of fish, and otherwise, lamentable and horrible to report, destroy the same, to the great hindrance and decay of the commonwealth.

Plus ça change . . . Fish conservationists have been pleading a similar cause ever since. The Elizabethans tried to settle the matter by a total ban on the taking of young fish by 'any manner of net, weele, but, taining, kepper, line, crele, raw, fagnet, trolnet, trimboat, stallboat, weblister, seur, lammet, or with any device or engine made of hair, wool, line, or camias, or shall use any haling net or trimboat, or by any other device, engine, cawtel, ways or means whatsoever'—what one might term a comprehensive list. It also gives an idea of what a complex and elaborate business fishing had become by the end of the medieval period. One other form of edible river life was covered by even more stringent regulations.

Chaucer's monk who had the taste for a swan, roasted whole, probably had no right to be tasting the bird at all. The swan was a royal bird, theoretically reserved for the royal table. However, the king did grant some important institutions the right to keep swans, and two London Companies, the Dyers and the Vintners, were granted that right in the 1470s—and they have kept it to the present day. Each group or 'game' of swans is given its own cygninota, the mark of ownership. Royal swans are left unmarked, Dyers' swans have a single nick in the beak, Vintners' two nicks. This marking is carried out each year as it has been for the last five hundred years in the ceremony known as swan hopping or swan upping. In July, when the cygnets are grown to a reasonable size, the Swan Wardens of the two Companies meet the Royal Bargemaster and his Swanherdsmen and make their way up river to Henley. The royal barge—in these days a modest skiff—carries the royal flag and a banner showing a swan with raised wings: the other boats each have banners with the Company crest. The wardens and herdsmen then have to face the far from simple task of catching, identifying and marking the swans and cygnets. Swan upping takes a full week of dawn-to-dusk working. The ancient ceremony also acts as a reminder that there is official protection for this most beautiful of birds, which has been hymned by poets from Milton:

> The swan with arched neck
> Between her white wings mantling, proudly rows
> Her state with oary feet

to Keats who, in one couplet, has caught all the majesty of the bird:

64

Oft have you seen a swan superbly frowning,
And with proud breast his own white shadow crowning.

Activity on and around the river had become a complex affair, and was to become more so. By the time the Wars of the Roses had finally been resolved on Bosworth field, and the Tudors had taken over the throne of England, the whole of Britain had entered into a period of rapid change and development which was to touch all aspects of life.

CHAPTER FOUR

A time of change

Anyone wanting to understand what sort of changes were brought about in those two dramatic centuries from 1500 to 1700 could get a very good idea of what it was all about by looking at the river scene. The two great symbols of medieval power, the monastery and the castle, were to fall: Henry VIII dissolved the monasteries, Cromwell destroyed the castles. For centuries, they had been the largest and most impressive buildings dominating the river scene, and quite suddenly this was no longer so. Both were reduced to ruins, but though they were to decay, elsewhere there were signs of new life and growth. For one river flowing through the heart of a major city there was to be an age of bustle and activity, splendour and pageantry, which would never be matched again. The river was the Thames; the city, London.

For Europeans, the world was getting larger all the time. In 1492, Columbus sailed to America, and six years later Vasco de Gama anchored off the Indian coast, after the first sea voyage to the sub-continent. It was the start of a great age of exploration, and a great age of maritime trade which was reflected in the busy ports of Europe. And few, if any, ports were busier than London. There were no closed docks, so boats were forced to anchor in the deep waters in the middle of the river, to be loaded and unloaded by lighters and barges. These were quite extraordinary craft, which must have required a good deal of skill to handle. The simplest lighters and dumb barges had no form of power at all, but simply went with the tide, being steered by large oars or sweeps. Primitive sailing barges were also to be seen on the river, rather like overgrown punts—simple square-sided boxes with overhanging bow and stern. The single mast was stepped slightly forward of midships, and could be raised or lowered by means of a winch or windlass in the bows to enable it to pass under bridges. There was a square sail and a minimal amount of rigging. Steering was by means of a long tiller, working a

66

square rudder. Where there was any accommodation at all, it consisted of a small cabin at the stern, with just enough room to sleep two. It was known as the cuddy. Between them, the lighters and the barges served their big sisters, keeping the river busy with their perpetual traffic. But they were by no means the only boats on the river.

London, in those days, could boast a river well stocked with fish. Henry VIII was presented with a polar bear which was kept at the Tower and led down to the river to fish for salmon. More orthodox fishers could be found all the way along the river, most owning their own boats which were worked with the help of an apprentice. These young boys had a hard life, usually forced to sleep out rough on the boats to protect them from thieves. They were often beaten, and had to share with their masters the vagaries of an uncertain trade. They also had to face competition from another type of fisherman—the fish merchant who brought his fish round the coast, importing such luxuries as salmon from the Tweed. These men sold to the wholesalers of Billingsgate who, in turn, passed the fish on to the mongers and hawkers of London.

Yet all this still only represented a fraction of the traffic on London's river. Until the eighteenth century, the Thames was only crossed by the one London Bridge, the famous medieval structure, topped with houses. It was, as John Stow commented in his London Survey of 1598, 'rather a continuall streete than a bridge'. In fact, it must often have seemed more of a barrier to progress than a useful way of crossing from one bank to the other. For many Londoners, the river itself became the main thoroughfare, on which boats of all kinds plied for hire. The most numerous of these aquatic taxis were the wherries, smaller versions of the river barges, powered by six or eight oars. Then there were the small 'skullers' or 'oars', worked by one man. The boatmen used to stand by the various sets of steps, shouting out 'oars, oars'—a cry which was misinterpreted by a visiting Frenchman, who was somewhat disappointed to discover he was being offered a sixpenny trip on the river and not the services of a lady of pleasure. These watermen plied their trade across the river and up and down its length. Any reader of contemporary accounts, such as Pepys' *Diaries*, will be struck by the frequency with which Londoners took to the water.

Travelling down the Thames could have its adventurous side, particularly if one wanted to go under London Bridge. The wide, fast-flowing river was squeezed between the narrow arches, where the water raced and eddied, making steering a hazardous business. Those who were brave enough to

shoot the central arch were able to dine out afterwards on stories of 'water
piled up . . . to a much greater height than we in our little ship', as one
traveller put it. Not every barge and wherry that attempted the passage
made it safely through. Old London Bridge was undoubtedly picturesque,
but it was a confounded nuisance to all river users.

The watermen themselves had something of a mixed reputation among
their customers, and even in the seventeenth century they were facing
competition from the growing number of road carriages. They did, however,
have one great champion in the wherryman turned poet, John Taylor. He
put their case in a poem, *An Arrant Thief* (1622):

> All sorts of men work all the means they can,
> To make a Thief of every waterman:
> And as it were in one consent they join,
> To trot the land i' th' dirt, and save their coin . . .
> Against the ground, we stand and knock our heels,
> Whilst all our profit runs away on wheels.

Taylor argued all his life in favour of water carriage against land carriage,
even objecting to the building of theatres on the north bank of the river
instead of on the traditional theatre ground of the south bank, on the basis
that it would reduce traffic across the river. The theatre did, in the course of
time, acknowledge its debt to the watermen. Thomas Doggett, the manager
of Drury Lane, died in 1721 and in his will left a sum to provide a Coat and
Badge, a prize to be raced for every year by young watermen, who were
required to row from London Bridge to Chelsea. Doggett's Coat and Badge
are still raced for every year in the oldest rowing competition in Britain. Such
trophies were some compensation for what the watermen regarded as unfair
competition. They were subjected to strict rules and regulations that did not
apply to their land-based competitors.

The watermen's rules were laid down by the Company of Watermen and
Lightermen. An abstract of these rules, published in 1708, shows just how
closely the Company sought to control river traffic. Watermen could, for
example, take as many apprentices as they liked, but no apprentice could
take charge of a boat 'till he hath Rowed two Years with an able Waterman'.
There were rules about plying for hire, which tried to prevent arguments by
forbidding boatmen from trying to coax away 'any Person about to take
Water with another', and passengers were protected from pestering boatmen by the establishment of specific plying places.

Lightermen had their own set of rules which, among other matters, tried to control the awkward passage through London Bridge. Only one lighter at a time was allowed through except at high tide, and anyone trying to get through on the flood who got himself grounded was fined five shillings. These regulations give a good idea of the sort of sharp practices found on the river: one does not, after all, have to ban something which never occurs. So, for example, a lighterman who bought coal from one of the coasters down from the Tyne or the Wear and then tried to pass it off as coal of a higher quality had to give forty shillings to the poor. Nobbling the competition was also frowned upon: 'He that loosens another's Lighter from his proper Foot, shall make good the Dammage sustain'd and forfeit 5s and make Satisfaction to the Party wrong'd'.

A high standard of conduct was expected of the watermen. They were not to work on Sundays without special permission of the Justices, nor were they to 'Swear, Curse, Revile, or Ply, or Work when Drunk; or suffer a Drunken Fare to work with both Skulls'. However, a pamphlet written at the same time as the rules, *A Kind Caution to Watermen*, suggests that expectations were not always met. Travelling by water, claims the writer, you can hear 'men bellowing out their lewd and filthy jests, treating one another with all the approbious language their Wit can invent and in pretence of being but in jest all the while, uttering those things, that are not fair to be nam'd among Christians'. John Taylor would, no doubt, have disputed such a view and, even if he could not claim that all boatmen maintained a high moral tone at all times, he could at least point out that they did their job well and at very low cost:

A waterman cannot be false to his trade for he has no weights or measures to falsify, nor can he curtail a man's passage: his worst fault is, that like a lawyer he will take more than his fee . . . his bare fee he will take willingly (upon necessity) but less than his fare, or many times nothing, me thinks goes against the stomach.

The fares were very reasonable. Those listed in the 1708 rules give the price of a crossing from London Bridge to Limehouse as twopence a sculler, while you could take a boat all the way from London to Windsor for fourteen shillings, with extra passengers only paying two shillings each. This compares favourably with some hand-written notes in the back of the Bodleian Library copy of the rules, which give the carriage fare from Haymarket to Red Lion Square as 1s 6d.

The boats were both popular and useful, so popular in fact that for big occasions every boat would be booked on the whole river. Samuel Pepys recorded in his diary for 23 August 1662 that he tried to get a boat to see King Charles II bring his queen to London from Hampton Court. 'I offered eight shillings for a boat to attend me for the afternoon, and they would not.' He was able, however, to get a splendid view of the whole pageant from the top of the new Banqueting Hall. 'Anon come the King and Queen in a barge under a canopy with 1,000 barges and boats I know, for we could see no water for them.' Those watermen had grimmer business four years later when the Great Fire devastated the city. Pepys again went to see and record the scene.

> Every body endeavouring to remove their goods, and flinging into the river, or bringing them into lighters that lay off; poor people staying in their houses as long as till the very fire touched them, and then running into boats, or clambering from one pair of stairs by the water-side to another. . . . River full of lighters and boats taking in goods, and good goods swimming in the water and only I observed that hardly one lighter or boat in three that has the goods of a house in, but there was a pair of Virginalls in it.

The Great Fire was mercifully an isolated event: the great winter freeze-ups were all too common in the seventeenth century. It was a mixture of unusually cold weather and the reduction in the river's flow caused by the obstruction of London Bridge that caused the phenomenon of London's river turning to ice. It was considered great fun by everyone except the boatmen but, being ingenious men, they soon found a way round their problems. After all, they had the right to charge those who wanted to cross their river. The fact that those who wanted to cross could now walk over without the help of a boatman had nothing whatsoever to do with the matter. The boatmen set up booths and charged the pedestrians the usual fare for the crossing. Most people seem to have thought the experience was worth the price, anyway, and the Frost Fairs became tremendous attractions. There were stalls and ox roasts on the ice, entertainments were laid on and the whole thing became so popular that even the royal family took to the ice, and the king slept out for the night in a special pavilion.

At this period, the Thames may have been the London river, but it was not London's only river, nor the only one to be put to use. Tributaries ran into the Thames at roughly three-mile intervals throughout the London area, though many of them are now out of sight, pushed underground to act as drains and sewers. Some were already sewers in practice, even when they were navigable rivers in name. The best known of these was the Fleet, which was used a great deal in medieval times but was much given to silting. In 1502, it was dredged 'so that boats with fish and fewel were rowed to Fleete Bridge, and to Oldbourne Bridge, as they of old time had been accustomed, which was a great commodity to all the inhabitants of that part of the city'. That state of affairs did not last. The playwright Ben Jonson, in his *Epigrammes* of 1616, described the unhappy effect of a boatman meeting the mud of the Fleet:

> Which, when their oares did once stirre,
> Belch'd forth an ayre, as hot as at the muster
> Of all your night-tubs, when the carts doe cluster,
> Who shall discharge first his merd-urinous load.

The Great Fire did at least provide the opportunity for some major town planning, and Christopher Wren drew up a plan for transforming the merd-urinous Fleet into a broad canal crossed by handsome bridges. The scheme went the way of the others. The broad canal took up valuable land and soon it was built over and restored to its earlier function as unofficial town drain. By the beginning of the eighteenth century, according to a few lines of doggerel in the *Tatler*, everything was going into the Fleet:

> Sweepings from butchers' stalls, dung, guts, and blood,
> Drown'd puppies, shaking sprats, all drenched in mud,
> Dead cats, and turnip tops, come tumbling down the flood.

In spite of this, people could actually be seen bathing in the Fleet, as an astonished Alexander Pope recorded in the *Dunciad*:

> The King of Dykes! Than whom no sluice of mud,
> With deeper sable blots the silver flood.
> Here strip my children! Here at once leap in,
> Here brave who best can dash through thick and thin,
> And the most in lure of dirt excel,
> Or dark dexterity of groping well.

Yet still the Thames itself managed to stay moderately fresh and clear and, in its upper reaches, it provided a welcome relief from the busy, workaday world of the city. This is the Thames described in one of the first and loveliest descriptions of river scenery, Edmund Spenser's *Prothalamion*, written in 1598 to celebrate the double wedding of the Earl of Worcester's daughters. The poet, tired of his 'long fruitless stay in Princes Court':

Walkt forth to ease my payne
Along the shoare of silver streaming Themmes;
Whose rutty Bancke, the which his River hemmes,
Was paynted all with variable flowers,
And all the meades adorned with daintie gemmes
Fit to deck maydens bowres,
And crowne their Paramours
Against the Brydale day, which is not long:
Sweet Themmes! runne softly, till I end my song.

Spenser's Thames is idyllic, the banks coated with violets, daisies, lilies and primroses, while swans glide past on the water. John Taylor took a more practical, if still poetical, view of the upper Thames. He was far less concerned with the flowers on the bank than with the sand banks and shoals under the water. His long narrative poem, *The Description of Thames and Isis* (1632) sets out very clearly where his main concerns lie:

But I (from Oxford) down to Staines will slide,
And tell the rivers wrongs which I espide.

The river which Taylor travelled was very different from the Thames we know today. It was almost totally undredged. Below Oxford, he found 'weeds, shelves and shoales all waterlesse and flat', while at Abingdon the shoals were even worse than at Oxford. The locks he met with along the way were not the sort we are familiar with on present-day rivers and canals, but flash locks, staunches and navigation weirs—all essentially similar devices, given different names in different parts of the country. A river such as the Thames had many of these devices simply because it had many weirs: there were fishing weirs built in a V with a trap at the apex and mill weirs serving a variety of different mills. The problem was the same at all of them—how to get the boat over the weir. The simplest and most common solution was the flash lock.

Two solid baulks of timber spanned a gap in the weir. The lower, usually of elm, was fixed solidly on the river bed. The upper was movable. It was above water level and could be pivoted or lifted clear. Between the upper and lower beams were a number of vertical timbers called rimers, and against these rested wooden paddles with long handles. When a boat was to pass, the paddles were pulled up, the rimers removed and the top timber swung out of the way. The water which had been dammed up behind the weir poured through in a torrent or 'flash', and boats going downhill rode down on the flood, like canoes shooting the rapids. Those travelling upstream had to be laboriously hauled up against the current, often by means of a winch. The flash certainly speeded boats on their way downstream, sometimes a little too rapidly for comfort, as Taylor discovered on his journey:

> Then Sutton locks are great impediments,
> The waters fall with such great violence,
> Thence downe to Cullam, streame runs quicke and quicker,
> Yet we rub'd twice a ground for want of liquor.

At least he did get safely through. Other users of flash locks were less fortunate. In 1634, a passenger boat with about sixty men, women and children on board overturned in the flash at Goring. There were no survivors.

Tragedies such as at Goring were fortunately rare, but delays at flash locks were all too common. The release of a flash would seriously disturb the work of the mill, so the mill owner, who controlled the weir, was most reluctant to let boats through. It was common practice to wait until there was a whole convoy that could be sent through at the same time. Astonishingly, such locks were in use right into the late nineteenth century on the Thames above Oxford, and Robertson in his book on upper Thames life described the frustrations of the boatmen—and the steps they took to overcome them:

> When the water is low, the river is flashed twice a week by the regularly appointed keepers of the weirs, each of them waiting till the water from the weir next up the stream has reached him. By this means a continually augmenting volume of water descends, on the flood of which the whole traffic is carried. Sometimes the bargemen are sorely tempted to draw a flash on their own account, when they may have been unusually delayed.

Such private enterprise was dealt with by a £20 fine in Robertson's time—provided the offenders were caught. Then, at least, such flash locks were a rarity, whereas in Taylor's day they dominated the river. The needs of miller and boatmen sometimes seemed irreconcilable and Taylor had no doubt where his sympathies lay:

> Haules Weare doth almost cross the river all,
> Making the passage straight and very small,
> How can that man be counted a good liver
> That for his private use will stop a river?

73

The weir was only one of the hazards facing the boatmen. At Clifton, Taylor found rocks, sand and flats 'which made us wade, and wet like drowned rats'. Even bridges provided unexpected obstacles, especially when the builders had become somewhat wayward in their line:

> We came where Chertsey's crooked bridge doth stand,
> Which sore was made all by left-handed men,
> The like of it was never in my ken;
> Win waw to Oakam ward, kim kam, kiw waw,
> That through it men can hardly set or row.

Taylor's list of faults that he found in his journey from Oxford is long and detailed. Yet this, as he claims, was the premier river of the country, giving employment to thousands and carrying a substantial part of the nation's trade; and carrying it very efficiently. As he pointed out, one barge with eight strong men to haul it could carry as much as forty carts. The river, he declared, was of vital importance and should be improved:

> There's many a Seaman, many a Navigator,
> Waterman, fishers, bargemen on this water,
> Themselves and families beyond compare,
> In number more than hundred thousand are,
> Who doe their Prince and Country often serve,
> And wer't not for this river might go starve;
> And for the good to England it hath done,
> Shall it to spoyle and ruine be let runne?

Taylor's was by no means the only voice raised in favour of river works, nor was the Thames the only river being proposed for improvement. Andrew Yarranton published a book in 1677, *England's Improvement by Sea and Land*, in which he joined Taylor in deploring the state of the Thames where 'many times the Barges lye on ground three weeks or a month together for want of water'. His solution was to dam up the Cherwell, or Sharwell as he called it, and release flashes of water in the dry season. Similar flashes would also come from the Kennet at Reading. He then turned his eye to other rivers. He was very keen to see work done on the Warwickshire Avon, which would help to turn Stratford into a major port and a manufacturing centre. His model, as with many advocates of water transport, was the Dutch, and his two industrial centres at Stratford were given Dutch names—'new Brunswick', where there were to be granaries and brewhouses for making Brunswick beer, and 'new Haarlem' for linen manufacture. That scheme came to nothing, but elsewhere he proved a more accurate prophet. Having

74

seen the extensive silting up of the River Dee, he foretold the end of Chester's importance as an inland port and correctly named its successor: 'the Trade of Chester is much decayed, and gone to Liverpool: and that old great City in danger of being ruin'd if the River Dee be not made Navigable by Act of Parliament, and Ships brought to the City'.

Francis Mathew was another eager pamphleteer. He proposed extending navigation from Lynn to Yarmouth by joining and improving the Little Ouse and the Waveney: 'What a blessing and ease would this afford to all the Inhabitants near adjoining, upon all Market daies to carry themselves and their Commodities by Water (avoiding those deep Waies in the Winter season, especially on Suffolk side).' That was only part of a general scheme to revitalize the waterways of the north-east, by restoring such ancient navigations as the Foss Dyke. Once, says Mathew, a king's barque might have sailed its waters, 'but what an unworthy neglect thereof hath been in these latter times I blush to write'.

He put forward an even more ambitious scheme in 1670 for joining Bristol to London by water. This would involve making the Avon navigable as far as Calne or Malmesbury, and then making an artificial cutting to join the Thames at Lechlade. It was, he agreed, an ambitious project, too ambitious for any private individual, so he presented his plan to king and government. 'I humbly presume, upon this stock, to become Importunate to Your most Excellent and Royal Majesty for the enterprise of and ready effecting this Work, being an Undertaking so Heroick, that 'tis beyond the levels of any others to attempt.' The king was, however, disinclined to attempt it; others did, though not quite along the lines suggested by Mathew, and more than a century was to go by before Bristol and London were joined by an inland navigation. Few of the schemes put forward by Taylor, Yarranton, Mathew and others actually came to early fruition, but they did create a climate of opinion in which later plans could develop. And a start was made even in their own day.

Among the first of the active river improvers was Arnold Spencer of Bedfordshire, who received a Patent from Charles I authorizing him to improve the Great Ouse between St Ives and St Neots. He built 'sluices' or 'staunches', which were similar in principle to the flash locks, except that they had just one big, heavy paddle which was winched up vertically in a wooden frame, rather like a guillotine. The Civil War did little to improve the quality of navigation on the river, but in 1674 the Ashley family took over and not only restored Spencer's work but greatly improved it.

75

The staunches on the Ouse were all very well in their way, but real improvement depended on the introduction of the pound lock—the device we know today simply as 'the lock'. It consists of a watertight chamber, closed at either end by gates, which can be emptied or filled through culverts closed by movable paddles. The earliest example in Britain seems to have been built on the Exeter Canal in the 1560s. The River Exe was improved by the construction of an artificial cut to by-pass shoals, with three locks to lift boats up to the Exeter level. The lock was improved over the years, and the next recorded example, built on the Lea at Waltham Abbey in the 1570s, set a pattern that was to be followed right up to the present. It was built with mitre gates at both ends: that is, a pair of gates which met in a V, being held together by water pressure.

The pound lock was a vast improvement over the old flash locks. It needed far less water and the rate of descent could be controlled, while the rising water lifted the boat uphill without the use of a winch. When Taylor made his voyage, there were three such locks on the Thames—at Iffley, Sandford and Swift Ditch. But for the finest of seventeenth-century navigation works you needed to take a turn down a tributary of the Thames, the Wey, which was transformed into a splendid waterway in the 1650s. Ten locks were built between Guildford and the Thames, and there were seven miles of artificial cuttings.

Many of these improved rivers were navigable by even the largest ships of the day, and their inland ports became ideal centres for shipbuilding. The requirements were very different from those of the later shipyards on the Tyne and the Clyde, for here the principal raw material was wood, and especially oak. The old song 'Hearts of oak are our ships' had a quite literal meaning: it was a wood with the virtues needed for shipbuilding—'tough, bending well, strong and not too heavy, nor easily admitting water'. That description was written by the diarist John Evelyn in a tract *Sylvia* published in 1664. Thanks largely to his advocacy, 11,000 acres of woodland in the Forest of Dean were enclosed and planted with oak. Young straight trees would be used for planks; older, twisted trees for 'compass', or curved timbers, for ribs and the like. It might seem a huge acreage, but not quite so large when you consider that no less than sixty acres of mature trees were needed for a single man o' war.

Chepstow, close to the forest and on the navigable Wye, was well situated to take advantage of the times. By the end of the seventeenth century, the local yards were kept busy with orders for the navy—the first recorded man o' war from Chepstow, 300 tons and capable of mounting up to thirty guns, was aptly named *Forester*. Sadly for the local shipbuilders, the government proved a fickle employer and when they ran out of funds at the end of the century, the unhappy builders found themselves in the debtors' prison. There was, however, other trade to be had in ships for Bristol's merchant fleet, trows for the Severn trade, and there was even money to be made out of serving the opposition. The Chepstow builders made barges to carry Dean timber to other yards.

The seventeenth-century dockyard was a plain, simple sort of place. Once the riverside site had been selected, far enough from the sea to be safe from gale, tempest and enemy raider, all that was required in the way of construction was a storehouse for the timber and a dock for the vessel. The docks were either dug down or partially built up with brick and timber walls. The space was pumped clear of water and closed off, not to be opened again until the launching day arrived. Naval architects drew up plans from which models were made, but shipbuilding was a very inexact science. Many shipwrights stuck to copying their last success and kept their plans secret. They were often little better than semi-literate. John Evelyn went to see the launching of the *Charles* at Deptford in 1668, and described its builder as 'old Shish, a plain honest carpenter, master builder of this dock, but one who can give very little account of his art by discourse, and is hardly capable of reading, yet of great ability in his calling. The family have been ship carpenters in this yard above 300 years.'

Work began with the laying of the keel, to which was attached stem post and stern post. The floor was laid, followed by the futtocks, the curved sides of the ship. So, the vessel began to take shape and staging was put up all round the hull as work continued. A busy yard would be surrounded by other activities. There would be rope walks, where great lengths of rope were made up by entwining individual threads, sail-making, block-making, painting. All these subsidiary activities made for a varied scene, yet the sites today can seem almost insignificant. It requires a major effort of imagination, for example, to see Buckler's Hard on the Beaulieu River as an important shipbuilding centre. Yet that is just what it was, developed to take advantage of the New Forest timber just as Chepstow looked to the timber from the Forest of Dean. And what a brave sight it must have made, when a great man o' war was launched out on to these lovely waters.

By the end of the seventeenth century, there were pamphleteers in plenty to shout the benefits of river improvement, and enough examples of successful schemes to make their plans seem practical as well as desirable. Yet, at the same time, the other river users were growing in number, and their demands often seemed to be in direct opposition to those of the boatmen. Water power, which had at first been almost exclusively limited to milling grain, was developing myriad new uses.

Well in the forefront of the new users were those of the rapidly developing woollen cloth industry. They made an extensive use of water power, but the river played an important part in the process even before the wool left the sheep's back. The animals had to be given regular washings to free them from ticks and other parasites, and the simplest way to get this done was to immerse the beasts in the nearest river. In many parts, sections of the river were closed off to make it easier to control the sheep. Elsewhere all you needed was a river, two strong men and a good supply of soap. This woollen industry had its very own poet in John Dyer, whose poem *The Fleece*, although written in the eighteenth century, describes a way of working that had not changed for centuries. The whole poem is something of a curiosity—a verse description of an industrial process. It is rather as if a modern versifier had set out to describe the Ford works at Dagenham, and had been at great pains to get the technical details right. Here is Dyer's pleasant and easy-flowing description of sheep washing:

> On the bank
> Of a clean river, gently drive the flock,
> And plunge them one by one into the flood:
> Plunged in the flood, not long the struggler sinks,
> With his white flakes that glisten thro' the tides;
> The sturdy rustic, in the middle wave,
> Awaits to see him rising; one arm bears
> His lifted head above the simple stream,
> While the full clammy fleece the other laves
> Around, laborious, with repeated toil;
> And then resigns him to the sunny bank,
> Where, bleating loud, he shakes his dripping locks.

This is a description of a scene by a man who knows it well, far removed from the idealized pastorals so beloved of Dyer's contemporaries, whose shepherds have little to do all day beyond wooing shepherdesses. It represents, however, only one small item in the long story of turning fleece into cloth. In this long tale, the river appears again only at the end of the narrative. The wool is spun into yarn, the yarn woven into cloth and the cloth cleaned from the grease of the machinery. It then had to be thickened and shrunk, and the cloth would, in fact, shrink to something like two-thirds of the width it had been when it left the loom. Now clearly the customer required that this alarming shrinkage should occur during the manufacturing process rather than when the cloth was on his back. These processes of thickening and shrinking were combined into one, known as fulling. From the early Renaissance onward this was carried out in specially built fulling mills. In the Middle Ages, before the introduction of machinery, the job was done not so much by hand as by foot. The fullers simply tramped up and down on the wet cloth, a process known as 'walking the cloth', and it is, in fact, the origin of the family name Walker. The fulling mill replaced foot power by water power.

The fulling mill was not the most pleasingly aromatic of work places. The initial process of scouring and cleaning the cloth was performed using a variety of different ingredients, from the relatively harmless fuller's earth to pig dung and stale urine. At one of the few surviving fulling mills in Britain that still retains its old machinery, Helmshore Higher Mill in Lancashire, there was a tradition that large vessels of urine were bought from the villagers. Long before the introduction of machines enabled the shy and coy to announce that they were off to spend a penny, the citizens of Helmshore could announce, with equal coyness but greater profit, that they were about to earn a penny.

In the mill, the walkers' feet were replaced by large wooden hammers, known as fulling stocks. The cloth, usually soaked in a mixture of soapy water and fuller's earth, was placed in a trough and pounded with wooden hammers, the heads of which were angled so that the cloth was moved in the trough with each stroke. The power from the stocks came from the water wheel, the rotating shaft being fitted with tappets which connected with the ends of the stocks. The hammer was lifted by the tappet, then, as it cleared, the hammer head fell back into place. By the end of the seventeenth century, such mills were almost as common as corn mills and, in the great cloth-making regions, they were even thicker on the ground. Celia Fiennes, an aristocratic lady possessed of an altogether admirable sense of curiosity, made a tour round Britain on horseback in the 1690s, and was ready and eager to poke her nose into everybody's business. Among the areas she visited was Exeter, which was then the centre for serge manufacture. The whole area for some twenty miles around the city was kept busy with the trade which, according to Celia Fiennes, 'turns the most money in a week of any thing in England. One week with another there is £10,000 paid in ready

79

money, sometimes £15,000.' She called in to see a mill at work, and was most impressed by the sight:

> It is a pretty diversion to see it—a sort of huge notched timbers like great teeth. . . . The mill draws in with such a great violence that if one stands near it and it catch a bit of your garment, it would be ready to draw in the garment in a trice.

After fulling, the cloth was taken out to the fields to dry, suspended in frames by means of tenter hooks—hence the well-known saying. The drying fields made a splendid sight with the great spreads of white cloth which were, according to Celia Fiennes, 'as thick set one by another as will permit the dresses to pass between, and huge large fields occupied this way almost all around the town, which is on the river side'.

This was the great age for West of England cloth manufacture, and tiny rivers which today must seem to have no conceivable use to man became power sources for whole strings of mills. Take, for example, the Gloucestershire Frome in the Stroud area, and follow the river from Chalford to Stonehouse. You will pass something like forty mill sites, each one representing a water-powered mill, its wheels turned by the waters of the same River Frome. Many of these mills have been altered or replaced over the years, but the majority of present-day mills stand on sites which have been occupied since the early sixteenth century. It was a prosperous trade, as the houses of the mill owners testify. Elegant and large, these houses placed their owners in the same financial category as the established squirearchy, even if the money did come from trade. Money could not always be relied on to buy a place in the local hierarchy—but it often did.

The use of rivers to turn the machinery of the fulling mills was not without its problems. Theoretically, there is no limit to the number of mills that can be turned by a single river, since the water that turns one mill is not used up in the way that fuel is used up, but simply passes on to the next mill down the line. This would appear to be a recipe for perpetual motion, but the actuality was not that simple. For a water wheel to work, there must be a considerable head of pressure above the wheel, and some energy is necessarily dissipated at each mill. Perpetual motion is a dream that can never become a reality. That head of pressure was maintained by holding back the river water in mill stream and mill pond, and if the mill upstream held back too much, then there might not be enough available for the next mill down the line. It was

Two views of eighteenth-century London:
Above: Old London Bridge which formed a major
obstacle to river traffic.
Below: The entrance to the River Fleet showing
typical Thames traffic.

The old London Bridge and the new bridge under
construction in 1830.

The iron bridge across the River Wear, Sunderland, in 1798.

Goole docks in 1905.

The industrial revolution brought a new look to the river frontage:
Abbey Cloth Mills at Bradford-on-Avon, designed and built in
1874 by Richard Gane for £18,000. The building was restored in
1971 having ceased to accommodate a cloth mill in 1902.

Fulling stocks at Otterburn Mills. The fulling process (or more accurately the felting process) involved the beating of soaked wool under large hammers which eventually changed the makeup of the fibre, forming a thicker material.

not unknown for feuds between rival millers to go on for years. At St Mary's Mill, between Brimscombe and Chalford, the weir was actually destroyed by Mr Iles, the owner of the next mill down the river, because he claimed he was not getting enough water passed on to fill his own pond. Eventually, the owner of St Mary's Mill agreed to lower the depth of water in his pond, and Iles paid twenty shillings to have the weir restored.

There was money to be made in the cloth trade. Thomas Baskerville, a visitor to the area in the 1680s, described the town of Painswick, three miles south of Stroud, in these terms:

> Here in this town you begin to enter the land of clothiers, who in these bourns building fair houses because of the conveniency of water so useful for their trade, do extend the country some miles, for they delight to live like the merry rooks and daws chattering and prating together, and if a man be able to purchase so much ground as will keep a horse or two yearly you shall have a house built there to spend £500 p.a. . . . and he that shall take a prospect of places where clothiers live, shall find the sides of the hills and country full of little grounds and paddocks.

The description still holds. There are still fine clothiers' houses, looking down on the river and the mill which brought prosperity. Not that it was always a prosperous time. The Civil War hit the cloth trade as it did everything else—not helped by Prince Rupert's requisition of huge quantities of material from the Stroudwater area to clothe his troops. He did, however, offer to pay the clothiers in full—adding that, unfortunately, all his funds were in Oxford. But if the clothiers would only call on him in that city they would get their cash—assuming that they could get there at all. Foreign competition, fluctuating trade—both affected the livelihood of the clothiers and their workers. Yet the industry prospered mightily, even if it was about to be overshadowed by developments in the north of England.

It is hard now to imagine the scene in those narrow, steep valleys radiating out like legs from a spider's body with, in this case, Stroud as that body. It must have been an extraordinary sight. All the way down the riverside, the busy wheels turned, and all round the mills the cloth was spread to dry. But where the fields around Exeter had been spread with white cloth, here the predominant colour was a spectacular scarlet, the famous brilliant red cloth of the Stroud area. Everywhere you looked, there was the scarlet cloth, filling every field between the prosperous houses. It was, in John Aubrey's words,

81

'A little Commonwealth of Cloathiers and Cloathworkers—not the like in the Nation'.

The big hammer of the fulling stocks falling on to cloth had a close relation in the big hammer of the forge. The iron industry, like the woollen industry, was growing rapidly, and changing its character throughout the sixteenth and seventeenth centuries. Many of the cloth mills have survived, offering direct evidence of a once thriving trade: the iron industry of the same period has left its mark in very different ways. The great centres of ironmaking existed in regions where today we can scarcely imagine any industry of any sort whatsoever existing. The valleys of the Taff, the Ebbw and the Rhymney were still part of a wilderness scarcely disturbed by man. Where the coal mines and the ironworks were to burgeon in the Industrial Revolution, then it was empty apart from a few hardy hill farmers. Not until the 1560s did the first ironmakers appear in the valleys of South Wales, and then only as a tentative venture in an attempt to escape a number of petty restrictions that had been imposed in the major centres—the Wealdland of Kent and Sussex.

Ironmaking in the Weald goes back to Roman times, but the use of water power only came in during the sixteenth century. Iron occurs naturally in Britain, mainly as haematite or blackband iron, but in either case it consists of iron in the form of the oxide. To get the metal you need to get rid of the oxygen, and this is done by heating with carbon. The sixteenth-century iron masters discovered that excellent metal could be produced by heating the ore with charcoal in a furnace kept at a high temperature by a blast of air. These furnaces were massive structures, so something a little more elaborate than a blacksmith's bellows was called for, and the answer came, yet again, in the form of water power. The Weald had all the right ingredients for the new process—wood for charcoal-making, iron ore and water for power. Unfortunately, one of the ingredients was not quite up to the standard of the rest. The rivers, such as the Arun and the Teise, are comparatively minor affairs, so a good deal of ingenuity was applied to solving the problem of supplying a good head of water—and keeping it all the year round.

Anyone walking or driving through the Weald gets the impression of a landscape of woods punctuated with charming little lakes. A glance at the Ordnance Survey map will show that these lakes have names such as Hammer Pond, Furnace Pond and New Pond. A wander round such a pond will result in the discovery that water runs out one end of the pond through man-made sluices while, at the opposite end, there is a dam across the little feeder river. These ponds which now seem so natural and peaceful were made by man, who dammed the river to provide a reservoir to feed the water wheels of the ironworks. These wheels turned to power the bellows and the hammers of the forge. Often the succession of ponds threaded along the length of a little river like pearls on a string are all that remain of one of the great industries of the past. Yet here they made fire grates and cannon balls, ornamental ironwork for estate gates, plain iron for horseshoes and nails. At Bayham Abbey near Tunbridge Wells, an important ironworks was established following the destruction of the monastery by Henry VIII. It is one of the very few such places to be commemorated in verse, and rather good verse at that. In *Puck of Pook's Hill*, Rudyard Kipling looked back from an industrial age to what seemed a Golden Age in the distant past, yet still found a place to remember Bayham and the iron industry of the Weald:

> And mark you where the ivy clings
> To Bayham's mouldering walls?
> O there we cast the stout railings
> That stand around St Paul's.
>
> See you the dimpled track that runs
> All hollow through the wheat?
> O that was where they hauled the guns
> That smote King Philip's fleet.
>
> (Out of the Weald, the secret Weald,
> Man sent in ancient years
> The horse-shoes red at Flodden Field,
> The arrows at Poitiers!)

Kipling looked back to a pre-industrial past, yet already there were signs, as at Bayham, of the industrial future. The growth of the iron industry along the little rivers of the Weald was so rapid that it was soon a cause of some concern. Charcoal burners were decimating the woods and in an attempt to save valuable stocks of timber, a Royal edict was passed, banning charcoal-making in the region. Sussex ironmasters went off in search of new areas to begin the industry again, and in 1564 they established an ironworks at Tongwynlais in the Taff valley, just north of Cardiff. The industrialization of Wales had begun, and it soon spread beyond what we think of as the traditional industrial areas of South Wales. The waters of the Wye were set to work turning over the hammers of forges set in the shadow of the ruined abbey at Tintern. Today, it is even more difficult to think of the Wye valley as an industrial centre than it is to imagine ironworks in the Weald, yet if you hunt in the woods and along the tributary streams, you can still find the decayed remains of blast furnaces and the pits where the water wheels once turned.

Even by the end of the seventeenth century, however, industrialization scarcely touched the majority of Britain's rivers. For most, the nearest thing to an industrial unit was the local corn mill and the waters carried nothing more grandiose than a rowing boat or lumbering ferry. There was, however, one other class of citizen to be seen on the banks of the rivers. This was the first great age of the angler: or, to put it another way, it was the age of the first great angler, Izaak Walton. Not that Walton was the first to extol the pleasures of rod and line. That honour belongs to Dame Juliana Berners, who published her *Treatyse of Fysshynge wyth an Angle* in 1496. In it she spoke for all anglers when she wrote: 'And if the angler take fysshe, surely thenne is there no man merier than he is in his spyryte.' She did not begin any great fashion for writing books on fishing, since a whole century was to pass before the next important treatise, Gervase Markham's *The Young Sportsman's Instructor*, and then fishing was only one of a number of activities described, such as hunting, hawking and trapping. It is, however, full of practical advice, though how useful the advice might have been to contemporary anglers is not always easy to determine. Take, for example, Gervase's recipe for a nice tempting paste. He suggests that to such familiar ingredients as bread, cheese and honey you might care to add 'Assa Foetida, Oculus Indiae, Oyl of Pelipody of the Oak, and the Gum of Ivy'. These are not quite the ingredients you can pick up at the local supermarket, while even the specialist shopkeeper might raise an eyebrow were you to enquire after the necessities for Markham's ointment, which rarely fails—'man's fat and the fat of the thigh-bone of a heron'.

Fly fishing was already in vogue, and every true practitioner was expected to assemble his own lures. Markham supplied this basic list of essentials to get the young sportsman started:

> Fur, Feathers, Wool, Down, Silk, Worsted, Bear's Hair, Camel's Hair, Badger's Hair, Spaniel's Hair, Dog's Hair, Sheeps Wooll, Mo-hair, Cow-hair, Camlets, Furs, Hackles or Feathers of a Cock's neck or tail of several colours, Silk of all Colours, Wire and Twist, Silver Twist, Gold Twist, Silver and Gold Wyre.

Such books were no more than preludes to the main work, *The Compleat Angler*, first published in 1653. It is an extraordinary book, a ragbag of homilies on everyday life and practical notes on fishing, a mixture of poetry and prose, anecdote and advice. Its appeal to later generations lies not so much in its practical hints as in its discursive sections, its picture of a rural idyll, far removed from a world just beginning to feel the crowding-in of industry. It is a pastoral, but a peculiarly British pastoral, offering an earthy Eden, populated not by lovesick swains and nymphs, but by honest countrymen, red-faced from sun and wind, who ask nothing more than a day by the river in the perennial battle with perch, chub, trout and salmon. Walton offers a 'compleat' life for his 'compleat' angler, recognizing that the pleasures of the sport extend beyond the business of landing fish. At the end of the day, Walton and his friends make for the village pub to talk over the day's catch and plan for bigger and better things for the morrow. The day ends with a sing-song round the fire, with hearty congratulations from Walton to the singer.

Well remembered, brother Peter, these verses come seasonably, and we thank you heartily. Come, we will all join together, my host and all, and sing my scholar's catch over again; and then each man drink the tother cup, and to bed; and thank God we have a dry house over our heads.

Walton himself was always ready, literally, to sing the praises of his sport. He quotes many different poets, and adds verses of his own which have the same virtues as the rest of his writing. They are honest, bluff and unsophisticated, but shot through with true enthusiasm for the subject:

> As inward love breeds outward talk,
> The hound some praise, and some the hawk,
> Some better pleas'd with private sport,
> Use tennis, some a mistress court:
>   But these delights I neither wish,
>   Nor envy, while I freely fish.

> Who hunts, doth oft in danger ride;
> Who hawks, lures oft both far and wide
> Who use game shall often prove
> A loser; but who falls in love,
>   Is fetter'd in fond Cupid's snare:
>   My angle breeds me no such care.

85

Of recreations there is none
So free as fishing is alone;
All other pastimes do no less
Than mind and body both possess:
My hand alone my work can do,
So I can fish and study too.

By no means all nor even a major part of the book is taken up with descriptive writing and verse. The heart of all is the practical advice from a practical man. If you wish to catch bream then, Walton tells us, 'he will bite at a grasshopper with his legs nipt off, in June and July'. And the advice goes beyond the business of catching the fish. He makes sure you make the most of your catch. Who could resist pike roasted with anchovies and oysters, or fail to agree with Walton's own description of it: 'This dish of meat is too good for any but anglers, or very honest men'?

The Compleat Angler was not an immediate success. In fact, it owes its fame to its rediscovery in the early nineteenth century, since when it has been reprinted more than 200 times. Nor did everyone approve of either the man or his sport. Byron, for one, took a very jaundiced view:

Whatever Izaak Walton sings or says;
The quaint, old, cruel coxcomb, in his gullet
Should have a hook, and a small trout to pull it.

Most of us, however, would be more inclined to go along with William Hazlitt, though it seems somewhat narrow-minded on his part to exclude both the Scots and the Welsh from his description. Hazlitt praised both the book and the activity which inspired it:

The English nation are naturally 'brothers of the angle'. This pursuit implies just that mixture of patience and pastime, of vacancy and thoughtfulness, of idleness and business, of pleasure and of pain, which is suited to the genius of an Englishman, and, as I suspect, of no one else to the same degree.

For those of us who live in the twentieth century, the great charm of Walton's masterpiece lies in its very ordinariness. We can still recognize the pleasures he describes. Fishermen still sit on the river bank, preparing their own very personal recipes for bait—always guaranteed infallible. They still wait for the twitch on the line, while their thoughts wander where they will. And they still gather in the country pub to swap tales with other anglers. Walton would be as much at home in that company as he was among his friends in Dovedale 300 years ago. But in his time, there were more rivers to fish and fewer restrictions on the fishermen. As the seventeenth century ended, not only a new century but a new age began. The world of the river and the river user was to change dramatically. If we think in terms of the amount of use man made of rivers, the amount of attention rivers received and the interest they evoked, then you could say that the rivers of Britain were about to enter into their Golden Age.

CHAPTER FIVE

The Golden Age

During the eighteenth century, the river life of Britain was busier than it had ever been before or would be again. Many of the activities were simply extensions of developments begun in earlier periods, yet, paradoxically, this was also to be the age when men turned increasingly to the delights of the untamed river. The Georgians discovered scenery.

The enjoyment of scenery is very largely dependent on the viewer having the leisure to look around and take in its beauties. To those who look at the land as the means by which they can eke out a living, however meagre, then the countryside is judged by what it will produce. So a stretch of river is assessed in terms of the trade it will carry or the fish it will yield. Only when you are independent of necessities can you sit back and enjoy the play of light on a stream or the dramatic effect of a waterfall. Not that the many who were entirely dependent on unremitting labour were oblivious to beauty. It is simply that it had a low priority in the struggle for existence, and however much they might appreciate their surroundings they had little time for quiet contemplation and none at all for lengthy discussions over which scenery was the most attractive. The leisured classes of the eighteenth century had the time, and their inclination was to discuss scenery at length and in quite a new way.

The key word in the enthusiast's lexicon was 'picturesque' which meant, quite literally, capable of being attractively portrayed in a picture. In a sense that begs the question, since virtually any natural phenomenon can be presented on canvas. The proponents of the picturesque had, in fact, a very particular type of picture in mind, and not even a British picture at that. The model was based in part on Poussin, but more especially on the French painter Claude Lorraine, who ranged even further afield, drawing his own inspiration from the countryside around Rome. It was a grand landscape of hills, rivers and trees—and, just as importantly, a landscape full of reminders of the past. The picturesque landscape represented a balancing act between darkness and light, order and disorder, the present day and the distant past. The solid mass of a castle, dark and mysteriously brooding, contrasted with the sparkle of water on river or lake. Strict regularity and formality were taboo: an old wizened oak was infinitely preferable to a formal avenue of regimented dullness; a comfortable modern house was nothing when compared with an ivied ruin. The British who went off on the Grand Tour of Europe were able to see Lorraine's originals. Others looked for the same elements nearer home.

The leading proponent of the cult of the picturesque was a clergyman, William Gilpin, whose first, and most influential, book was *Observations on the River Wye*. It is difficult for the modern reader to see quite why it should have been so popular, since Mr Gilpin's prose style is distinctly turgid. The other difficulty comes from our own view of scenery. We should not be in the least surprised to read a passage such as this in a modern guidebook: the language may be somewhat archaic but the opinion is unremarkable:

> After sailing four miles from Ross, we came to Goodrich Castle; where a very grand view presented itself; and we rested on our oars to examine it. A reach of the river forming a noble bay, is spread before the eye. The bank on the right is steep, and covered with wood; beyond which a bold promontory shoots out, crowned with a castle, rising among the trees. This view, which is one of the grandest on the river, I should not scruple to call *correctly picturesque*.

Unremarkable to us, but to the eighteenth-century reader such opinions were literally eye-openers. People began to stare at such scenes and see them as beautiful, even if in a very specialized way. Gilpin's view of the 'correctly picturesque' was strict, and unaided nature was by no means up to the task of fulfilling all requirements: 'She is an admirable colourist; and can harmonise her tints with infinite variety, and inimitable beauty; but is seldom so correct in composition, as to produce a harmonious whole.' So, the castle, the man-made, had its place, providing a focal point to the view. Yet even the ruin was required to meet Gilpin's strict rules. Travelling on downriver he came to Tintern which, one would have thought, would have answered perfectly. Not so, declared Gilpin, there is too much order here, not enough ruin. 'A number of gable-ends hurt the eye with their regularity; and disgust by the vulgarity of their shape. A mallett, judiciously used (but who durst use it?) might be of service in fracturing some of them.' Fortunately, Mr

89

Gilpin himself did not dare to attack the great abbey and travellers reluctantly had to accept the scene as they found it. The great landowners, however, had no such restrictions. If the scene from their windows was insufficiently picturesque, then they had the power to change it.

The eighteenth century was the great age of landscape gardening, and the major planners such as William Kent, Sir John Vanburgh and Capability Brown all made use of rivers and water in their schemes. The advantages of water in a garden were expounded as early as 1677, when John Woolridge produced his book, *The Art of Gardening*:

> Although small Crystalline Springs brought in Pipes may be sufficient to irrigate your Groves and Plants, and supply your Grotts and Fountains and add very much to the splendor of your Garden; yet a Fair stream or Current flowing through or near your Garden may add much to the Glory, and pleasure of it. On the banks of it you may plant several aquatick Exoticks, & have your seats or places of repose under their Umbrage, and there satiate your self with the view of the Curling Stream and its nimble Inhabitants.

A splendid example of just such a garden can be seen at Rousham, where the Cherwell runs at the bottom of the grounds. William Kent designed this beautiful and very natural-seeming park to provide both riverside walks and classical pavilions where the owners and their friends could sit and watch the curling stream go by. Some five miles away another gardener took a different view of what nature had provided. The grounds at Blenheim were laid out by Capability Brown. The tiny River Glyme ran through the valley, but was not sufficiently attractive to meet Brown's needs. He wanted something altogether grander as the centrepiece for his park. He dammed the river to form a large lake in front of the house, and then sent the water on its way again down a suitably picturesque, if entirely artificial, waterfall at the southern end of the lake. Now he had the basic ingredients to construct his three-dimensional Poussin or Lorraine. All that he needed to add was the classical Roman touch, and that was quickly provided by the handsome bridge across the lake.

Many of the new generations of landscape gardeners found that a river crossed by a suitably designed bridge was the ideal ingredient to add the classical touch. One of the finest examples is at Wilton House in Wiltshire where Roger Morris designed a superb Palladian bridge to cross the River Nadder. It is large and handsome, topped by a colonnade. Space did not always allow for anything on that scale, but if a bridge was needed then the designers made sure a bridge was provided. At Kenwood House in London, the bridge does indeed make the scene but is, alas, a sham—a façade put there purely for its visual appeal. There is no denying that it, and its more useful and grander brethren, have just the right effect in producing a landscape which, if not a direct copy of one of the picturesque paintings, does perfectly capture the spirit. An anonymous poet expressed this view in a work published in 1767 with the cumbersome title *The Rise and Progress of The Present Taste in Planting Parks, Pleasure Grounds, Gardens, Etc.*

> But your great Artist, like the source of light
> Gilds every Scene with beauty and delight;
> At Blenheim, Croome, and Caversham we trace
> Salvator's Wildness, Claud's enlivening grace,
> Cascades and Lakes as fine as Risdde drew,
> While Nature's vary'd in each charming view.

Those without the means to create their own domestic wilderness who did have the means to travel, set off eagerly in search of the picturesque scene. To an earlier age, when pleasures derived from scenery were directly related to the scenery's usefulness, the Thames was the ideal river, busy and profitable. The tourists turned their gaze in quite different directions. For them, the ideals were represented by rivers such as the Wye and the Dove. The attractions of Dovedale are obvious, but if today it sometimes seems impossible to catch a glimpse of the scenery at all through the crowds of tourists, then we are doing no more than following where the Georgian travellers led. Nowadays, however, we have become a little blasé about the natural landscape. We are very unlikely ever to match the extravagant enthusiasm of the Georgian traveller seeing Cauldron Snout in Teesdale for the first time:

> The awful and tremendous grandeur of the sight that arrests your attention, is almost more than the mind can bear. The painful, pleasing experience of heart—that internal sensation and best criterion of the true sublime—seizes you with instantaneous and overwhelming energy. Directly before you, the river is hurled headlong from rock to rock, in a deep recess, down the declivity of a mountain, all but perpendicular, for several hundred feet: and if it is possible that the horror of this scene can be aggravated, it is so by the uncouth aspect of the surrounding objects.

Waterfalls were obvious tourist attractions and many of them, such as the Clyde Falls in Scotland and Rheidol in Wales, were seldom short of visitors.

But the visitor could find another aspect of eighteenth-century river life intruding on his view. John Byng, Viscount Torrington, went to see the equally famous Aysgarth Falls on the River Ure. After admiring the falls themselves, he wandered off to view the nearby ruins of Nappa House, and contemplated the prospect of rebuilding the place. Settled in such a home, away from the world of business and commerce, 'a man might here enjoy fly-fishing and grouse shooting in the highest perfection'. Musing happily on this prospect, he walked on his way round a bend of the river and there, brash and new, stood a cotton mill and 'on the instant it completed the destruction of every rural thought'. The modern world and the new life of the river had caught up with him.

The traditional woollen industry of Britain was still thriving, but increasing wealth brought an increasing demand for finer materials. Silks were imported, largely from Italy, and the native merchants began to think of producing their own cloth. There was already a substantial colony of silk weavers in England, drawn from the ranks of Huguenot refugees, but the silk thread itself had to be imported. But, argued the merchants, if we could only manufacture the thread as well, we could be self-reliant—and make far larger profits.

There were early attempts to establish silk mills, where the yarn could be spun by machinery powered by water, by two inventors, Thomas Cotchett and George Sorocold. The latter, in particular, is one of the unsung heroes of the Industrial Revolution, a man who did more than any other to establish the practicality of the water-powered factory. But, as is often the case, it is not the pioneers who are remembered, but the men who made the inventions into commercial successes—and in the silk industry that means Sir Thomas Lombe and, to a lesser extent, his brother John.

Now it seems most likely that the Lombes borrowed some ideas from Cotchett and Sorocold and got the rest from an Italian book published in Padua in 1607, and available in Britain some twenty years later, describing silk-spinning machinery. That, however, makes for a dull tale, and there is a much more exciting account available. In this version, John Lombe visited Italy in disguise and managed to wangle his way into an Italian silk works. This would make him the world's first industrial espionage agent, for he surreptitiously noted down all the details of the spinning machinery. He then scurried back to brother Thomas, a wealthy silk merchant, who built the machines and a new factory to house them.

Here, at least, we can get back to the facts, for Thomas Lombe did indeed establish a water-powered silk mill on an island in the River Derwent at Derby. In 1718, he was granted a patent for 'a new invention of three sorts of engines never before made or used in Great Britain, one to wind the finest raw silk, another to spin and the other to twist the finest Italian raw silk into organzine in great perfection, which was never before done in this country'. The new silk-spinning machinery was powered by a water wheel, turned by the Derwent. Lombe's new installation has a fair claim to the title of Britain's first factory, and because it was powered in the same way as the familiar corn mills were powered, it too came to be known as a mill. The name stuck, and has been applied to textile factories ever since.

John Lombe died only three years after the mill had begun operation, and after his death the stories surrounding his exploits became even more colourful. The silk manufacturers of Piedmont, discovering that Lombe had taken their secret back to England, where the new mill threatened Italian trade, sent their own agent after him. This agent, an eighteenth-century Mata Hari, was given a more sinister task than mere espionage. The beautiful young lady soon won her way into the Lombe household, where she proceeded slowly and systematically to poison the unfortunate gentleman. So, the Piedmontese had their revenge. All very melodramatic, but not, it appears, very plausible, so we are left with the more mundane story of the establishment of a new process and the beginning of the factory age. The silk mill led to little activity, and brought no very dramatic changes to society. The same could certainly not be said of the next move to harness the power of Britain's rivers for the service of industry.

Silk is expensive, and necessarily had and has a limited market. Wool, the traditional cloth of Britain, is excellent, but heavy and, on the whole, rather plain. But the expansion of trade had brought a new type of cloth from India. The East India Company had been formed in 1599 and, finding that the Dutch had a virtual monopoly of the spice trade from the islands of the East Indies, looked for a suitable trading commodity on the Indian mainland. They found a cheap, lightweight cloth which could be printed in brightly coloured patterns. They sent samples out from their base in Calcutta and named the cloth Calico. The material was made from cotton.

Cotton cloth was immensely popular with everyone except, that is, the wool manufacturers. They used every argument to have it banned, from cries of economic woe and despair that would follow on the destruction of the trade, to mockery of those who chose to wear 'Indian carpets' on their backs. For a while they were successful, but legislation proved less powerful than fashion. As the novelist, Daniel Defoe, himself an ardent propagandist for the woollen trade was forced to admit: 'All the Kings and Parliaments that have been or shall be, cannot govern our Fancies: They may make Laws, and shew you the Reason of those Laws for your Good, but two Things among us are too ungovernable, *viz* our Passions and our Fashions.' He concluded, somewhat regretfully, 'The ladies will wear what they please, and dress how they please.' He was right. Cotton had arrived.

If cotton was wanted, then cotton would be supplied, but British manufacturers saw no good reason why India and the East India Company should make the profits. The race was on to design machinery for spinning cotton quickly and economically in Britain—and it was won by Richard Arkwright. He designed machinery for spinning cotton into thread and because the machines were powered by water they became known as water frames. They worked most satisfactorily, but Arkwright was still faced with a number of problems, all or any of which could get in the way of his main objective, which was to make a fortune for Richard Arkwright. The experience of previous inventors in the textile industry had shown what fate could lie in store for the rash and incautious. They had found themselves caught in a pincer attack: on one side were the traditional workers who saw the new machines as a threat to their livelihoods, on the other were rival manufacturers. The first smashed the machines; the second cashed in on the new idea, with no regard for such petty restrictions as the patent laws. Either way, the inventor lost out. The answer lay in secrecy. But how do you set about establishing a big factory worked by revolutionary new techniques without letting anyone else know what you are doing? Arkwright's solution was to find a spot where there was some tradition of textile working, yet which was remote from the major centres of Yorkshire, Lancashire and the West of England. He went to Derbyshire and the hamlet of Cromford and there, on the banks of the Derwent, he built his mill.

Everything was done that could be done to keep matters quiet until he was ready to bring his new cotton thread on to the market. No one was to be admitted to the mill, and locks were ordered for every door. Advertisements were put in local papers for locksmiths, blacksmiths, millwrights and others who were familiar with either water power or working with machinery. The machines themselves were simple enough: the cotton was pulled out into long fibres by being passed through rollers moving at different speeds, and was then twisted into thread. Simple though they were, they all had to be built up from scratch. But Arkwright had to provide more than mill and machinery. Having selected this remote spot, he now had to build a town to house his new workforce. The mill was the first cotton factory, Cromford the first cotton town.

It was all an immediate success, in the sense that Arkwright could produce cotton yarn in a quantity and at a price which no competitor could match. More mills were built around Cromford, while Arkwright's business partners, the Strutt family, built their own mills further down the Derwent at Belper. These early mills were tall, narrow buildings. The water wheel turned a horizontal shaft and, as in the grain mill, this was geared to a vertical shaft, which carried power to the different floors of the mill. This, in turn, moved overhead shafts passing the full length of the building, from which belts passed down to the rows of machines. In the cottages of the textile district, spinsters still worked at their wheels, each spinster producing a single thread from a single spindle. Now, a many-handed giant had appeared. There was still one wheel, but now it was turned by water and from it a thousand spindles turned, producing a thousand threads. The new mills marked the end of the old ways. A new world, based on the factory, had arrived. It seemed that nothing could now halt the move towards a new concept of ever-expanding production. Certainly, Arkwright saw no reason why the change should not be pushed ahead with all the speed he could manage. He had started life as a poor barber. He was now wealthy and wanted to be wealthier still.

Arkwright's notions of secrecy could not last for long. Everyone wanted to see the new wonder. Tourists who had dashed off to enjoy picturesque views of the Wye now rushed to the no less picturesque Derwent, though their interest was all centred on the marvellous new mills. The factory was even celebrated in verse by Dr Erasmus Darwin—medical man, scientist and poet. His lines are not always easy to understand today, though they seemed more appropriate two hundred years ago. Classicism was all the rage and the Classical allusion was considered appropriate for any description, even if it was the description of a textile factory. Here is Darwin describing Arkwright's mill and water wheel, which were turning the fibre from the cotton plant, *Gossypium*, into yarn.

> Where Derwent guides his dusky floods
> Through vaulted mountains and a night of woods
> The nymph Gossypia treads the velvet sod,
> And warms with rosy smiles the wart'y god;
> His pond'rous oars to slender spindles turn,

> And pours o'er mossy wheels his foaming urns;
> With playful charms her hoary lover wins,
> And wields his trident, while the Monarch spins.

Arkwright continued to build new mills, and began to license other industrialists to use his patented machines. These, in turn, became tourist attractions, especially one mill begun on the Clyde by David Dale. Here was a double attraction: the splendid and beautiful Corra Linn falls, and the village and cotton mills of New Lanark. The Duke of Rutland in his journal of a tour in the north of Britain in 1796 rhapsodized over the town and David Dale's benevolence:

> We are struck by the excellence of his arrangements with regard to the health, order and morals of his work-people, in which his benevolence, no less than his good sense, was obvious. His plan must indeed be considered a model, and it furnishes a convincing proof that most of the objections to manufactures on the score of their injurious influence on the persons employed in them, may be obviated by management and attention.

Those qualities were to be shown to an even greater degree by Dale's successor who was to make the name of New Lanark famous—Robert Owen.

Management and attention were not, however, always or even often forthcoming. The new machinery was largely worked by women and children, many of the latter being apprentices housed in specially constructed apprentice houses. With the introduction of gas lighting, mills such as Cromford could be worked twenty-four hours a day. The river, after all, ran for twenty-four hours a day, so there seemed little point in keeping expensive machinery idle when power to turn it was free. Shift followed shift in the mill. As one group of children climbed out of their beds, another group fell exhausted into them. They quite failed to share in the tourists' enthusiasm for the romantic sight of the mill lights gleaming across the water.

It could reasonably be argued that, in eighteenth-century Britain, the mill children were by no means the worst paid nor the worst treated. Against this one can say that men such as Arkwright made fortunes out of their labour and, in any case, the argument against the mills was not based simply or even mainly on a dislike of hard work and low pay. The new machine imposed a new work discipline. When the sluices were opened and water cascaded from the river to turn the wheel, then at that moment a thousand

and more spindles would start to turn, and they had to be tended. Old freedoms, slight though they may have been, were not simply eroded but lost altogether. Families could no longer choose for themselves when and how they worked. The machines turned as steadily and inexorably as the rivers that moved them. At first, however, there was little opposition. There was no great tradition of cotton spinning in the Derwent valley: these mills represented work for the poorest families, not a threat to old-established customs. Then the mills began to spread, and inevitably reached the traditional textile districts of Lancashire. Arkwright himself went into a partnership to build a mill on the river Yarrow at Chorley. The local spinners, seeing a threat to their old style of working in their own homes, rose up and marched on Arkwright's mill in October 1779. Another famous industrialist, the potter Josiah Wedgwood, was in the area and sent this account to his partner, Thomas Bentley:

> A capital engine, or mill, in the manner of Arcrites (*sic*) and in which he is a partner, near Chorley was attacked, but from its peculiar situation, they could approach it by one passage only, and this circumstance enabled the owner, with the assistance of a few neighbours to repulse the enemy, and preserve the mill for that time. Two of the mob were shot dead upon the spot, one drowned, and several wounded. The mob had no fire arms and did not expect so warm a reception. They were greatly exasperated and vowed revenge: accordingly they spent all Sunday and Monday morning, in collecting fire arms and ammunition and melting their pewter dishes into bullets. They were now joined by the D. of Bridgewater's colliers, and others, to the numbers, we were told, of eight thousand, and marched by beat of drum, and with colours flying to the mill where they met with a repulse on Saturday. They found Sir Richard Clayton guarding the place with 50 Invalids armed, but this handful were by no means a match for enraged thousands: they (the Invalids) therefore contented themselves with looking on, whilst the mob completely destroyed a set of mills valued at £10,000.

The mills of Lancashire fell, and the tall new buildings that had begun to line the river banks were now no more than blackened, worthless shells. Fear of the invading army of destroyers spread back into Derbyshire. Men were armed, defensive barriers set across the approach roads and, even today, visitors to Belper can see the gun embrasures cut into the bridge joining two of Strutt's mills. In the event, it proved to be a limited campaign: the invasion never came. The spinners went back to their homes, content with having rid Lancashire of its mills. It was a short-lived triumph, for the mills soon returned. In 1781, Richard Arkwright's patents for spinning machinery were challenged in court, and the challengers carried the day. Now anyone could build a mill and install the new machinery. It was too good an opportunity to miss, and the north-west of England and many parts of Scotland were engulfed in a wave of mill buildings. No river, no matter how sluggish and low, was considered to be insignificant. If there was any chance that its waters could work a mill, then work a mill they would. Inevitably some schemes started on paper and ended in the same place. Others were launched, floundered for a while in the economic shallows, then foundered and sank.

If you walk along the banks of one of these north-western rivers, even a comparatively minor one such as Hebden Water which flows down from the moors towards Hebden Bridge, you can see ample evidence of what the coming of the cotton mills did for the region. The river itself is scarcely more than a fast, bubbling stream, yet all along its course there are signs of industrialization, even in areas which today are chosen as quiet, scenic spots for a Sunday stroll. Within the town there is more than ample evidence of activity in the old mill buildings that still line the river, but as you walk out into the countryside, all that seems to be left behind. The area seems to be about as heavily industrialized as Dovedale. The rivers falls over broken rocks and on the banks there are flat, grassy areas—just the thing for an improvised game of cricket and a family picnic. Yet the broken stones are often the remnants of weirs, and those flat areas mark the foundations of the long-gone mills. One mill does, however, survive—Gibson mill, small and stone-built, with its mill pond behind it.

The valley is undeniably beautiful, and even the lonely survivor has the romantic charm that comes with advancing years. Yet the moss-covered stones can be a disguise for a squalid past. The big, gaunt multi-storey mills, such as those by the Derwent, were often far less cruel academies for the very young than the country mills along the Hebden. At Belper, at the end of the bridge over the Derwent, you can see the little house in which the Strutts set up a cottage hospital, and the top floor of North Mill was used as a schoolroom for the young apprentices. Gibson Mill is arguably more attractive to look at, but it was in the remote mills that the worst examples of brutality occurred. Such factories were often too small to be very profitable, so the owners tried to squeeze every last drop of effort from the few workers. It was in such arcadian surroundings that young boys and girls were regularly beaten, not for anything they had done wrong, but simply because nothing but pain could keep them awake through the long hours of drudgery. The discovery that the power of rivers could be harnessed to work the machinery of the new industrial age opened the way to a general increase in prosperity. One could see the prosperity throughout the country: one could not always see the pain.

Industry and transport are inseparable Siamese twins. The former cannot grow unless the means exist to feed it with raw materials and take the finished product away to the customers. Equally a transport system is very little use unless it has something to carry. Industry was, in the eighteenth century, able to supply cargoes in plenty, but was the transport system adequate to the task? The answer at the beginning of the century was, at best, a very highly qualified 'yes'.

Historians have, in the past, tended to look at road transport in this period and dismiss it as totally inadequate. There is certainly no shortage of comments from contemporaries to suggest that all was not quite what it might have been, but recent research has shown that things were not altogether grim. The historian, J. A. Chartres, for example, has analysed the trading patterns at three separate dates, and worked out what he calls a 'service quotient', produced by simply multiplying the number of services to a particular place by their weekly frequency. So that, for example, a service run by one trader which runs six times a week between Bedford and London scores six, and so would once-weekly services run by six different traders. The quotient reflects the fact that in both cases the customer gets his six services a week. Looking at trade out of London, we find road trade to the home counties doubling in less than a century—a quotient of 272 in 1637 reaching 372 in 1681 and leaping to 611 by 1715. However, an analysis of Chartres' figures shows a marked difference in pattern between the regions. There is a very strong emphasis on short hauls, with nearly half the total traffic from London going to the Home Counties and the South-East. There is also a difference in types of transport. For short runs, the bulk of the goods was carried in waggons, while for longer journeys the pack-horse was favoured. And pack-horses, as eighteenth-century engineers found out for themselves, were just about the least efficient means available for shifting heavy loads.

Towards the end of the century, several leading engineers got together to test just how much a single horse could shift by various means. The pack-horse came bottom of the league with a mere eighth of a ton. The stage waggon, running along the soft, muddy roads of the day, was a big improvement at five-eighths of a ton—but put your goods in a boat on the river and that same horse could shift thirty tons. These are remarkable figures, with one horse drawing a barge doing the work of 250 pack animals. At the beginning of the century, engineers may not have had such accurate experimental figures to draw on, but with that sort of startling difference in efficiency no one could have been unaware of the advantage of water over road transport. There was, however, one snag—the barge had to be able to move freely over the water. It was up to the engineers to provide the navigable routes.

River improvement had begun in the seventeenth century, and the same sort of work continued into the next. There was a great deal that could be done by such simple measures as dredging, piling the banks and cutting back weeds. Yet even more could be done by more ambitious men with grander notions. A new figure appeared on the river scene—the professional civil engineer. The name was not, in fact, applied until much later, but that nevertheless is what such gentlemen were. They were employed in making rivers navigable that had never been navigable before. They were so successful that where there had been only some 680 miles of navigable river in 1660, by the 1720s, the figure had risen to 1,160 miles. Typical of the ambitious schemes of the period was the plan for uniting parts of two rivers, the Aire and the Calder, improving them to make the Aire and Calder Navigation.

The Aire has its source high in the limestone hills of the Pennines, and could, indeed, be said to have the most dramatic beginning of any river in the British Isles. Where most rivers start life as an insignificant trickle over moorland or heath, the Aire starts at Malham Tarn, and then runs underground to emerge at the foot of the great overhanging cliffs of Malham Cove. From there, it makes its way down Airedale through a country more thickly populated with sheep than people, a circumstance which is not insignificant in view of the river's development for, by the time Skipton is reached, one has arrived at the mills of the busy woollen textile industry. Wool mills soon followed on cotton mills, and further up the valley were two of the major centres of the trade, Keighley and Leeds. The Calder begins its life in the Pennines above what was to become the cotton town of Todmorden, but soon, like the Aire, it flows through the woollen district, passing close to Halifax, then running on through Wakefield to join the Aire at Castleford. Joined together, the waters of the two rivers run down to the Humber and thence to the sea.

Given the differences between road and river transport, there was every incentive to give the Yorkshire woollen industry a watery route to the sea, which could be used by large vessels. In 1697, the engineer John Hadley, described by a contemporary as a 'great Master of Hydraulicks', set off to survey the Aire in company with the Mayor of Leeds and Ralph Thresby F.R.S. The latter noted in his diary that 'the ingenious Mr Hadley questions not its being done, and with less charge than expected, affirming it the noblest river he ever saw not already navigable'. So, in January 1698, Lord Fairfax introduced a bill to the House of Commons for making the rivers Aire and Calder navigable, the Aire from Leeds and the Calder from Wakefield. It was supported by petitions from all the major manufacturing centres. The Wakefield petition carried much the same message as that from Leeds, Halifax and the rest. It argued the case for cheap transport, and complained at length about the state of the local roads, since at that time goods had to be sent twenty-two miles to Rawcliffe, the nearest navigable point on the Aire, 'the expense whereof is not only very chargeable, but they are forced to stay two months sometimes while the roads are passable to market, and many times they receive considerable damage, through the badness of the roads by overturning'. There were voices raised against the proposals, notably the official voice of the mayor and commonalty of York, who saw the new navigation as a challenge and a threat to their own route via the Ouse to the same eventual outlet in the Humber. There was also a private complaint from Francis Nevill, who owned mills at Wakefield and feared the effect on the water power to his various concerns. The navigation was, however, approved, though only after lengthy argument, which at least kept the lawyers happy on both sides. Royal assent was given on 4 May 1699, sixteen months after the bill had first been presented to the Commons. So the actual building could, at last, get under way and was not to take very much longer, thus establishing a proud tradition in civil engineering, whereby the arguments take longer and cost more than the construction.

Hadley was appointed chief engineer for the project at what was for those days an exceedingly handsome salary of four hundred guineas a year. The Aire was already navigable as far upstream as Weeland and from there to Leeds it rose sixty-eight feet in thirty miles. The Calder rose twenty-eight feet in the twelve miles to Wakefield. Locks were built to overcome the difference in levels, ten on the Aire and four on the Calder. The size of the locks, 58 foot long by 15 foot wide, was determined by the type of vessel the builders expected to see using the waterway, the vessels already trading on the old navigable sections, the Humber keels.

The keels were, in many ways, the most primitive of all the sailing barges in use in Britain's inland waterways. They were clinker built, and fitted snugly into their new locks. They had a maximum draught of 5 foot 6 inches, and when fully loaded sat very low in the water. These bluff-bowed vessels were square-rigged, generally with a single sail on a mast stepped slightly forward of 'midships. Some keels also carried a small oblong topsail. Primitive they may have been in some respects, but they were sufficiently practical to keep going well into the twentieth century. Over the years, the life of the keelmen changed surprisingly little, and we have a wonderfully detailed and vivid account of this life from keelman Henry Fletcher, *A Life on the Humber*.

To describe the keels as sailing barges is technically accurate, but is only a part of the story. In the broad waters of the estuary they could run before the wind or tack against it, and a fully loaded keel, white sail stretched and decks awash, blunt bows pushing through the waves, made a brave sight. In the narrower parts of the river, the tall mast came into its own, holding the sail high to catch any breath of wind that was going. But the keelmen knew that if they had the wind at their backs going one way, it would be against them coming back again. Then the keel had to be moved by muscle power. The muscles could be those of a horse in charge of one of the 'horse marines' who plied for trade on the river. Such animals had a short and a miserable life. It took eight hours to pull a keel for ten miles, and it was a non-stop journey, with the animal getting its feed from a nosebag as it tramped along the towpath. If there was no wind and no horse, then it was the keelman and his family who had the task of hauling the heavy load. Some families lived on board and everyone, down to the very smallest, was expected to help out when needed. When running with the tide they could make good way, but steering was a difficult business. The keels ran through treacherous waters, often with strong tides whipping round banks and shallows. Accidents were all too common, and the keels carried a small dinghy, the coggy boat, which was the crew's lifeboat if, as could happen all too easily, the keel capsized. But the vessels themselves were splendid, as anyone who has seen the restored keel, *Comrade*, and its sister, the sloop, *Amy Howson*, can testify, even though one is aware that life aboard was far from glamorous.

The keels were only one variety of sailing barge, and the Aire and Calder was only one of a whole series of navigation improvement schemes that were brought in during the century. Each tended to follow the same pattern. A scheme was put forward, a bill promoted through Parliament and a Navigation Company formed. They financed the building work and ensured, they hoped, a return on the capital by levying tolls on boats using the new waterway. Charges varied considerably according to the goods carried. The Aire and Calder tolls were listed in an Act passed in 1774 for the improvement of the waterway. These varied from a charge of a halfpenny per ton per mile for 'Dung or Stable Manure' (though pigeon dung cost twice as much, for some reason, at one penny per ton per mile) to seven shillings for cloth bales. In between was a list of a whole range of goods, from grain to timber, coal to iron and chalk to cheese. There was thus a good deal of scope for fiddling the accounts, a favourite trick being to hide an expensive cargo under a cheaper—though whether there would be a ready market for best Cheshire cheese secreted under a pile of pigeon dung must be open to question. By the end of the century, there were many reports of wholesale pilfering by the boatmen on the river navigations—but as the claims were mostly made by those who were trying to promote the new generation of canals, they can hardly be described as unbiased. Slanging the opposition was a commonplace, just as the roads and land transport had been denigrated by the navigation promoters.

New river navigation companies were formed all over Britain, and a number of engineers made their reputations in such work, men such as William Jessop who was to go on to become one of the busiest and most successful engineers of the canal age, and John Smeaton, the famous builder of the Eddystone lighthouse. Smeaton was, it would seem, the first man to describe himself as a civil engineer. Though he well deserved his high reputation, he was not always blessed with good fortune in his river work. In 1757, when bad weather stopped work on the lighthouse, he set to work on the Calder and Hebble Navigation, which extended the Aire and Calder from Wakefield to near Halifax. Weather was to have an even worse effect down there than it had at Eddystone. Smeaton built no fewer than 26 locks in 24 miles of navigation, to overcome a level difference of 178 feet. He also constructed nearly six miles of new cutting, only to see all his work undone in one night. On 7 October 1758, torrential rain in the Pennines sent a great flood down the Calder valley. All Smeaton's work was washed away, the navigation was closed and the company ruined. It was not until 1769 that a new Act of Parliament was obtained, and a new company formed, so that work could start all over again.

Each navigation company went its own way. Matters such as lock size were determined entirely by the dimension of boats that worked the nearest stretch of the coast or estuary waters. At first, this made little difference to anyone. Then the navigation age gave way to the canal age, when navigations finally became divorced from the natural waterways. In 1760, the young Duke of Bridgewater, unable to get satisfactory terms for shipping his coal from his mines at Worsley into Manchester, simply gave up arguing and paid for a brand-new canal, which found its own route across country—so independent was it of natural rivers, that it actually flowed right across the River Irwell at Barton on Britain's first aqueduct. It marked the beginning of a new age, a vast opening up of the interior of the country to navigable waterways. It was to have an important effect on the development of river trade.

The canals spread across large parts of Britain, with a great concentration in the English Midlands. The early years were dominated by one man, James Brindley, the engineer who began working on the Bridgewater Canal and was to go on to become chief engineer for many other concerns. When he first built locks on the Bridgewater Canal, he did as his predecessors on the river navigations had done and looked at the types of vessels that would be likely to use the new waterway. Locks connected the canal to the Mersey at Runcorn, so he decided to build these to take a common variety of river boat, the Mersey flat. The locks were 72 foot long by 15 foot wide. However, when he came to work on the next batch of canals, those joining the Trent to the Mersey and on to the Severn and the Thames—a scheme known as The Cross—he decided that those original locks were too large. They needed a lot of water, and building his new canals to those dimensions involved other structures being built to the same size. On the Trent and Mersey, this would have involved building the one-and-three-quarter-mile-long Harecastle tunnel to accommodate boats 14 foot wide. This was a lot to ask of a primitive technology. So Brindley kept his locks to the same length as those at Runcorn, but halved the width. New boats were built to fit the new locks, a reversal of the traditional way of doing things, and the result was the emergence of what we now think of as the traditional boat of the inland waterway—the narrow boat. In the hey-day of canals these outnumbered all other types of vessel, yet still only represented one kind among an astonishing variety of craft.

Brindley set the gauge for the narrow canals which formed a unified system in the English Midlands, but around them all was confusion. The problems later engineers faced with broad gauge, narrow gauge and standard gauge railways were as nothing compared to the tangled web built up by the canal and navigation engineers. Narrow boats were too long for the north-east, broad boats too wide for the Midlands and there were a score of variations on the theme. Places which might never have had any significance grew up simply because they stood on the spot where different canal and river gauges met—Stourport, at the junction of the Severn and the Staffs and Worcester Canal; Shardlow, where the Trent and Mersey Canal met Trent Navigation; Sowerby Bridge, where the Calder and Hebble met the Huddersfield Canal. These inland ports looked to both river and canal, and were perpetually busy with a rich variety of boats. Now there were connections made between rivers at opposite ends of the country, but it was very rare to find a vessel which could traverse the entire system. It did, however, serve to bring new traffic to rivers once they were joined by an artificial canal. The two great rivers of Scotland, for example, the Forth and the Clyde, were joined by canal, and a major port was developed at Glasgow. Port Dundas was to form a nucleus for a whole new batch of industrial developments.

A traveller touring round Britain's rivers would have been impressed by two factors—the volume of trade and the diversity of the boats that carried it. Rivers and canals did not have their Bradshaw until long after the railway version had become indispensable to all serious railway travellers, but it finally appeared in 1904 and was compiled by Henry Rudolph de Salis, a director of one of the largest canal-carrying companies, Fellows, Morton and Clayton. In the introduction, he listed all the different types of boat to be found on inland waterways. In the section on non-sailing vessels, he mentions some 30 different types, varying in size from the big flats of the River Weaver, 90 foot long by 21 foot beam, capable of carrying 250 tons, to tub boats, which were simple metal boxes pulled along in a train, each box taking a maximum load of around 4 tons. The latter could be seen, for example, by the Severn at Coalport. They carried coal and ironstone for the furnaces up on top of the hill. They were loaded from boats on the Severn, then pulled along the Coalport Canal to the foot of a railed track. There they were floated on to wheeled bogies and hauled up the steep slope or incline, and then floated off their bogies on to a second canal at the top of the hill. The men of the eighteenth century could never have been blamed for a lack of inventiveness. There were fewer sailing vessels listed, but then de Salis' list was not comprehensive. In any case, the sailing boats, if fewer in number, were no less interesting.

Everyone no doubt has his particular favourites among the sailing boats using Britain's rivers, depending perhaps on which part of the country he knows best. There are plenty to choose from; though some, alas, are scarcely more than memories. The River Tamar, for example, had its own distinctive craft, the Tamar barge. This was a shallow draught vessel with a square transom stern, and a single mast, fore and aft, rigged with mainsail and foresail. This made sailing much simpler than with the square-rigged keels of the Humber. There was a busy traffic on the river in the eighteenth century: limestone, going downriver, sand being brought upriver for agricultural use. There was granite for building and coal being brought in to serve the needs of the mining industry in the upper valley. Once there was a major harbour complex at Morwellham, now an industrial museum, where goods were brought in on the Tavistock Canal, which served the local mines. The water has long since retreated from the wharves, leaving bollards standing sad and alone among weedy fields. Further downriver, in a beautiful wooded setting, is Cotehele quay where an old Tamar ketch has been restored.

Different craft have quite different appearances, and often handle in quite different ways. The Norfolk wherry, with its single gaff sail, is an unforgettable sight and, like all river craft, it has its own way of moving without sail. The single sail can be lowered by winch, and the mast itself can also be brought down, when necessary. After that the hard work starts, the boat being pushed along by a 24-foot pole or quant, a sort of punting on the grand scale. We can still see the wherry. Other craft, such as the sailing flats of the north-west that traded on the Mersey, the Irwell and the Weaver, have all vanished. The last of them, the 'Daresbury', was scheduled for restoration, but sadly never reached retirement let alone restoration: she sank.

Perhaps the best-loved and certainly the best-preserved of all river sailing craft are the barges of the Thames and Medway. One can trace the development of the Thames barge quite closely, from the old cross-sail barges that were common on the Thames in the seventeenth century. The main feature of these vessels is the spritsail. Unlike the square sail of the keels, the spritsail is self-adjusting and, being fore and aft rigged, can take the wind on both sides of the canvas. It can be seen in use on Dutch vessels in paintings and engravings dating back to the seventeenth century. The spritsail itself is abaft of the mast, and the sprit is a spar running diagonally upwards from a point part-way up the mast, extending the upper corner or peak of the sail. The rigging is necessarily more complex than with the square-sailed vessels. The heel of the sprit is secured in a rope collar, which has the rather odd name of 'snotter', which in turn is prevented from sliding straight down the mast by a rope from the mast head, the standing lift. The upper end of the sprit is secured by two ropes, the vangs, while the lower end of the sail is secured by a single sheet. The sail can be furled by pulling ropes attached to the edge of the sail, drawing it in towards the mast.

The spritsail was introduced to the Thames in the late seventeenth century, but the hulls were still simple floating boxes. By the eighteenth century, the barges had foresails as well as spritsails and leeboards had been added, pear-shaped boards which could be lowered into the water on either side of the vessel to stop it shifting sideways in the wind. Later, the swim bows, the sort of undercut bow you get on a punt, gave way to the more familiar pointed bows, though the vessels retained the transon stern. Sail was also increased, with a topsail and spanker being added. These, however, were much later developments. Chapman's *Architectura Navalis* of 1766 shows a Thames barge of 56 foot length and 15 foot beam which is still swim headed, and the same design can even be found as late as 1803, when the Admiralty sent out drawings of a barge as the basis for a flat-bottomed boat to be built in Port Jackson, New South Wales. The Thames barge certainly travelled a long way in its day.

The most distinctive feature of the Thames barge is its red sail, which developed from the original treatment of the sailcloth with an amalgam of horse-grease and tar, mixed with ochre, an unappetizing brew to form the basis for the most romantic sight to be seen on any river. The memory is still vivid of an evening in the late 1950s when the *Cambria*, the last of the commercial barges, came sailing up past Greenwich in the wake of a blood-red sunset that turned those sails to an even richer hue. It was a reminder, too, of what the river must have been like when the barges were thick on the water. They came in all kinds, carrying a variety of cargo, though the oddest of all were the hay barges bringing fodder to the working horse of London. The hay was piled as high as ten feet above the gunwales—and provided an ideal hiding-place for smuggled goods. Accidents were common on the busy river, particularly with those shooting London Bridge. In May 1798, a hay barge was late lowering its mast. It swung in the current, and the sprit hit the balustrade. The falling masonry injured a man and killed a small boy. The master could have lost his vessel as a result. Indeed, if a boatman fell off his barge and drowned, the vessel could be confiscated, for under the law the vessel was deemed to be an instrument that had caused a man's death and was forfeit to the Crown.

Life on the rivers was busy, but then so was life on the land. Road transport was also improving and that, in turn, produced a demand for more and better bridges across the rivers. Builders and architects responded with some magnificent structures. It might seem odd to think of architects in this connection, but the profession of engineer scarcely existed before the beginning of the eighteenth century and as a bridge is, after all, a form of building, it seemed logical to turn to a designer of buildings. There was, in any case, a strong feeling that a structure as important as a new bridge should show its importance by its sense of style. Nicholas Hawksmoor, the architect whose churches were and are among the glories of the city of London, wrote a pamphlet in 1736, *A Short Historical Account of London Bridge*, in which he put forward his own ideas for a new bridge across the Thames, based on Italian models, especially the work of Palladio. His ideas were never realized, but the classical style he advocated was used for a new bridge across the Thames at Blackfriars, designed by Robert Mylne, and for the new London Bridge, when it eventually appeared under the direction of John Rennie. The latter bridge now sits somewhat incongruously in the middle of Arizona.

Blackfriars Bridge marks an important breakthrough in British bridge design, for Mylne used the flat, elliptical arch instead of the semicircular or pointed arch of earlier builders. This meant firstly that arches could be built to a much greater width, so that bridges need no longer be as the old London Bridge was described in a pamphlet of 1756, 'barricades to trade'. The elliptical arch was also more graceful, and fitted in well with the popular classical style. Classicism was also carried over to the first stone to be laid at Blackfriars, which honoured in Latin both the designer Mylne and the leading man of the day, William Pitt. Unfortunately, it seems that the classical impulse was not matched by classical scholarship, and the inscription was roundly criticized and the author condemned as a man 'wholly ignorant of Classical Latinity, and an entire Stranger to the usual Stile of Inscriptions'. Then the critic Birch found himself, in turn, criticized, lampooned in a ballad 'The Antiquarian School', which mocked his outrage at the bad Blackfriars Latin.

> Busby Birch, true descendant of Busby the Great,
> A flogster most famous Historians relate;
> But this Fame when Compar'd with our Hero's but small
> For his Antiquarie has flogged ye all.

Whether Mr Busby's criticism was justified or mere pedantry, the classical style remained as popular as ever. There were even direct imitations of Italian originals transplanted to British soil, notably the imitation of the Bridge of Sighs, built across the Backs at Cambridge. And the same concern to build not only well but with a feeling for beauty and style was found in the most unlikely circumstances. The Jacobite rising in Scotland in 1715 had shown up the wretched state of the roads in that country and General Wade, given the task of pacifying the Highlands, put in hand a major road-building programme to facilitate troop movements. Yet even he looked for a touch of grace, and for his bridges he turned to the best and most talented designers he could find. In his own words, 'the best architect in Scotland was employed and master masons and carpenters sent from ye northern Countys of England'. The architect was William Adam, and he designed a magnificent five-arched bridge across the Tay at Aberfeldy, quite the finest structure to emerge from Wade's great rush of activity.

The classical style is the most distinctive mark of the bridges of this period, a mark which was to be carried over to those watery bridges, the aqueducts of the canal age. Yet even more important than stylistic changes were the technical advances made in construction. An early example can be seen in the Taff bridge at Pontypridd. A local mason, William Edwards, was given the task of building the road bridge across the river, and his early efforts were not entirely out-and-out successes. Bridge number one was washed away in a flood, and bridge number two collapsed under the weight of its own masonry. Thomas was faced with the problem of building a bridge strong enough to withstand flood, but light enough to avoid disastrous collapse of the stonework. He found a solution by piercing holes through the spandrils, the solid sections of masonry above the base of the bridge on the two banks. By leaving holes in this part, he could lighten the load without affecting the strength of the arch. So version number three was an unqualified success, and from 1756 when it was completed until 1831 when the new London Bridge was built, Edwards' bridge across the Taff could boast of having the widest span—at one hundred and fifty feet—of any bridge in Britain.

The real breakthrough in bridge design came, however, in 1779 when the world's first metal bridge was built over the Severn at Ironbridge. It was mostly the work of Abraham Darby III, head of the pioneering iron-making company at nearby Coalbrookdale. It was, and is, magnificent, crossing the river gorge in a single span of one hundred feet. It is, though, something of an anomaly, with the cast-iron members fastened together by mortice and dovetail joints as though they were baulks of timber. Anomaly it might have been, but here was a far simpler way of combining lightness and strength than anything Mr Edwards had been able to produce at Pontypridd—though curiously, there is an echo of that design in the roundels set above the iron ribs. It was a fine achievement in its own right, and an inspiration to the up-and-coming generation of engineers, particularly Thomas Telford. Before the Victorian age had begun, Telford had designed a number of spectacular iron bridges, of which the finest examples are in Scotland and Wales. The Craigellachie Bridge across the Spey shows an interesting if rather quirky mixture of styles: the iron span is as neat, elegant and modern as can be, but is flanked by stone towers decked out in the full Baronial style, with castellations and arrow-slits. No such mixture is seen at Betws-y-coed, where the simple bridge still carries a message, spread across the width of the arch: 'This arch was constructed in the same year the Battle of Waterloo was fought'. Telford was also partly responsible, together with the chief engineer of the project, William Jessop, for that other great Welsh river crossing—the aqueduct that carries the Llangollen branch of the Ellesmere Canal across the River Dee near Llangollen. This aqueduct, Pont Cysyllte, is the finest piece of civil engineering that the Georgian age ever produced.

One other river bridge deserves a special mention. It is quite an impressive structure with a span of 103 feet, which crosses the deep valley of the Houghwell Burn in County Durham. It carried neither road nor canal, but instead had a railed track along which colliery waggons were hauled by horses. It is the Causey Arch, completed in 1727 and the world's oldest surviving railway bridge. Almost a century was to pass before the horse was replaced by the steam locomotive, but once that had happened the railway age proper was born. It was to have a long-lasting effect on the future of the country's rivers.

CHAPTER SIX

The steam age

The steam railway is one obvious example of the way in which the arrival of steam power affected the life of the river, for it offered a fast, economical alternative to water transport. But the effect of the steam engine was felt long before the first locomotive tottered unsteadily down the tracks. Even before the eighteenth century had ended, the steam engine had begun to take over from the water wheel as the prime mover for industry.

The use of water power absolutely dictated the siting of early industries. They had to go where the water already existed. The use of the steam engine did not mean that the old mills were scrapped and industrialists rushed off around the country to hunt for new sites. That would have been nonsensical. The machinery was still there, there were workers who knew how to use it and, in any case, water power was both efficient and cheap. The old power did, however, suffer from the problems of drought, so it seemed only prudent to add a new engine to take over the work when water levels were too low to turn the wheel. Such 'belt and braces' caution spread even to quite small concerns, in fairly unlikely situations. The Blenheim estate in Oxfordshire had its own maintenance works, with carpenters' shop and a smithy. At one end of the building is a water wheel, turned by the Evenlode; at the other, a beam engine for use in dry spells. Such engines, of course, also need some water, both for steam-raising in the boiler and for condensing the steam, so they too are not unaffected by severe drought. Quite recently, the supply of water from the river to the condenser dried up, and within minutes the engine house was doing a passable imitation of a hyperactive Turkish Bath. Such events were, however, rare.

If the steam engine had been no more than a reliable back-up to the traditional water wheel, it would have had very little effect on the pattern of life in the industrial areas. That, however, was not the case. In the textile industry, where the effects were seen at their most dramatic, the necessity to use all available water sources had resulted in a curious phenomenon: what one might call octopus development. At the centre would be the town and radiating out from the town were the rivers and tributary streams, all supporting their complement of mills. Rawtenstall in Lancashire could be taken as an example. It stands on the River Irwell, which was lined with mills, far more than the small streams that fed it could possibly support. So you find the lesser streams supporting a few mills, which become increasingly isolated as you move away from the town centre. Instead of the continuous line of the major river mills, they are spread out at ever longer intervals, until they end up out in the empty moors where transport was both difficult and expensive. Inevitably, with time, the remote mills became unprofitable. In the past, there had been no choice—limited water resources were to be used to the full—now the old mills could be closed and new steam-powered mills built right in the town centre, close together for cheap transport and close to the homes of the workers. So the town mills grew and the country mills declined. Today one can walk out along little pathways and find the remains of the old mills. Sometimes the walls still stand, the remains of the wheel pit can be seen—often there is little more than a scarcely identifiable pile of stones. There is no mistaking the mill town, though, its skyline punctuated by tall chimneys. As for the rivers themselves, they were no longer so much used as misused.

The concentration of factories in the mill towns was accompanied by a great expansion of house building, though the latter description may seem all too grandiose to describe the way in which the slums were thrown together. Of all the towns which grew so rapidly and changed so dramatically, no town showed the new trends more clearly than Cottonopolis itself, Manchester. In 1842, a twenty-two-year-old German, son of a wealthy cotton manufacturer, was sent by his father to learn what he could from the British industrialists. Father must have been shocked when he discovered just what lessons the son was to absorb. The young man appears to have travelled through every street and alley in the city and he wrote descriptions of everything he saw. His name was Frederick Engels, and his book *The Condition of the Working Class in England*. It aroused, and still arouses, controversy. This is not the place to discuss the political conclusions that Engels and his friend Marx drew from the observations. But no one reading Engels' descriptions can doubt that what he described is what he saw. The rivers, which had been man's friend, now seemed his enemy. Here is his description of the Irk as seen from Ducie Bridge.

Marlow Lock with steam launch in the 1880s.

Henry Taunt, the great photographer of the Thames, beside
Wallingford Bridge.

Above: Wickerwork fish weirs being set up on the River Severn using techniques that have been in existence for a thousand years.

Right: Severn fishermen tarring nets in 1897.

Above: The Thames barge, one of the most successful and longest lasting of all the sailing barges.

Right: A Humber keel still afloat in the twentieth century.

A train of Tom Puddings taking coal to Goole.

A river steamer on the Severn pulling a convoy of narrow boats.

At the bottom flows, or rather stagnates, the Irk, a narrow, coal-black, foul-smelling stream, full of debris and refuse, which it deposits on the shallower right bank. In dry weather, a long string of the most disgusting, blackish-green, slime pools are left standing on this bank, from the depths of which bubbles of miasmatic gas constantly arise and give forth a stench unendurable even on the bridge forty or fifty feet above the surface of the stream. But besides this, the stream itself is checked every few paces by high weirs, behind which slime and refuse accumulate and rot in thick masses. Above the bridge are tanneries, bone mills, and gas-works, from which all drains and refuse find their way into the Irk, which receives further the contents of the neighbouring sewers and privies. It may be easily imagined, therefore, what sort of residue the stream deposits. Below the bridge you look upon the piles of debris, the refuse, filth, the offal from the courts on the steep left bank; here each house is packed close behind its neighbour and a piece of each is visible, all black, smoky, crumbling, ancient, with broken panes and window-frames. The background is furnished by old barrack-like factory buildings.

This was the Irk in the 1840s, the river along which people made such homes as they could, even being forced into cellars which, according to Engels, have floors 'at least two feet below the low-water level of the Irk that flows not six feet away from them'. No surprise to find such districts ravaged by epidemic diseases, and such conditions were by no means limited to Manchester. Industrial pollution affected the rivers from one end of the country to the other, from Taff to Clyde, Tees to Trent. No one in authority cared very much about it until the stench quite literally reached the nostrils of the Honourable Members at Westminster.

River pollution was not just the result of the expansion of industry, though that was one very obvious cause. Around the dye works of the textile industry, the evidence was inescapable, and even today one can find a river emerging from the midst of a huddle of nineteenth-century mills, tinged with a rich variety of hues. But pollution was also spreading because of the growth of population and the total lack of a proper sewage disposal system: the river, it was assumed, would take it all. There is a tale of Queen Victoria paying a visit to Cambridge, looking down from a bridge at the pieces of paper floating beneath, and enquiring what they were doing there. The Master of Trinity, being a quick-witted gentleman, replied with a deal of accuracy: 'Those, ma'am, are notices that bathing is forbidden.' If the Cam was bad, the Thames in London was atrocious.

Originally, the open sewers of London were intended only to take away storm water. Cess pools took the sewage, and these were regularly emptied and the contents taken away for use as fertilizer. The system lasted well enough for a time, but during the course of the eighteenth century, the population almost doubled to 1¼ million and a new sanitary device became available which actually made matters worse—the water closet. The contents of that went straight to the sewers. The cess pools were also soon overflowing, and in 1843, after a cholera outbreak, the Metropolitan Commissioners of Sewers were set up. They took drastic action. They abolished some 200,000 cess pools and put the households on to main sewers. But where did the sewage go? Straight down into the poor old Thames. That did very little to help anyone, and in 1848–9 there was a second cholera outbreak, even worse than the last, and 14,000 Londoners died. A lot of commissioners sat down and did a lot of talking, but no one seemed to have much of an idea what to do. The population was growing, and industry was spreading and adding its own twopennorth of muck. In 1855 one of the foremost scientists of the day, Michael Faraday, wrote a letter to that great repository of national indignation, *The Times*. He complained of the condition of the river, which he described as 'an opaque pale brown fluid'. Something, it was agreed, should be done, and this time there was a man on hand to do it: Joseph Bazalgette, the engineer who had been in charge of constructing the Victoria Embankment.

The Metropolitan Water Board, formed in 1855, handed the problem over to Bazalgette, who produced a set of proposals the following year, when a hot summer produced the Big Stink. Parliament, however, seemed none too anxious to push legislation through, and might never have authorized Bazalgette to go ahead had not the Year of the Big Stink been followed by Years of Even Bigger Stinks. 1858 was appalling and in 1859 the windows of Westminster were draped with curtains soaked in disinfectant in the vain hope that the aroma might be kept at bay. When at last it became clear to even the least sensitive nostrils that something had to be done, authorization was finally given for what was to be one of the great works of Victorian civil engineering.

In essence, the new scheme consisted of a whole system of sewers, running down to the river, but instead of discharging into the Thames they ran into main sewers, running parallel to the banks. These took the sewage to Barking on the north bank, Crossness on the south. There the solid matter was removed in settlement tanks and loaded into barges which carried it out to be dumped near the mouth of the river. The liquid was pumped out into the river at the beginning of the ebb tide, when it was hoped that the pollutants would all be carried out to sea where they would be harmless. Here the steam engine which had done so much to encourage the concentration of the population in towns was brought in to help solve the problem it had caused. Sewage works are not the most popular topic of discussion these days, but the Victorians were rightly proud of their achievement and they expressed that pride in the magnificence of the great pumping houses, such as that at Crossness. It was a veritable temple of sewage, ornate and spectacular, grand enough to serve as a palace for a king—grand enough, anyway, for Prince Albert himself to perform the opening ceremony.

Some decency returned to the Thames, though it is only recently that even firmer anti-pollution measures have restored life to London's river. Getting rid of waste was only one function of the rivers of Britain—supplying fresh water was another. Increased pollution was making that commodity somewhat rare. One answer was to build reservoirs, and here the various water authorities could draw on the experience of the canal engineers who had constructed many large reservoirs to feed their new waterways. Large they may have been, but they were nothing like as large as those needed to provide water for a city. Rivers were dammed and, as more and more water was needed, so the dams, which were no more than huge earthworks, rose higher and higher. In 1864, the inevitable happened. The hundred-foot-high Dale Dyke dam outside Sheffield gave way. Two hundred million gallons of water swept down into the valley, and 250 lives were lost. If huge reservoirs had to be constructed, then clearly different methods had to be found.

One of the most rapidly growing cities in Britain was Liverpool, and when the good citizens of England wanted water, they turned their eyes across the border to Wales. It was decided to dam the River Vyrnwy, and work began in 1881. It was a vast undertaking. The new dam was to be made of stone instead of earth, using blocks that weighed as much as 12 tons each. When the dam was finished it was over 1,000 foot long and 144 foot high, and as the waters rose they formed the largest artificial lake in Europe. The English had gained a reservoir of 12,000 million gallons of water; the Welsh had lost a valley. At least there was genuinely fresh water available for Britain, and again the steam pumps were brought in and kept busy supplying homes and industry. But the noise of the steam engine was not only heard beside the rivers: increasingly it was to be heard on the rivers as well.

The idea of using the steam engine to power a boat was around for a long time before anyone actually did anything about it. Thomas Savery, one of the pioneers of steam in the early eighteenth century, had a notion of putting a pumping engine on board a ship, but eventually gave up, saying, 'I dare not meddle with that matter.' Given the standards of boiler manufacture and its marked tendency towards explosion in his day, every sailor in Britain should have raised a prayer of thanksgiving at the news. And since the only steam engines then available were the hugely cumbersome beam engines, there was no shortage of practical difficulties facing the would-be inventor. There was, however, no shortage of triers, and there was an obvious model on hand for the actual propulsion system. If flowing water can turn the paddles of a water wheel then, logically, turning paddles can make water flow. The paddle boat was the predictable offspring of the water wheel.

The first successful experiments were not made on a British river. In 1783, a gentleman with a very impressive name, the Marquis Claude de Jouffroy d'Abbans, constructed a paddle steamer, the *Pyroscaphe*, which made a successful voyage up the river Saône. Around the same time, an American was busy experimenting with a different form of propulsion, and in 1787 James Rumsey designed a vessel which worked by means of a pumping engine. It drew in water at the bows of the boat and shot it out at the stern. Six years later, Londoners had the chance to view this extraordinary jet-propelled steamer, when it was given a trial on the Thames. No one seemed especially enthusiastic, nor even very interested and the development of steam power was, in any case, severely handicapped by James Watt's patent which effectively barred all experiments, except those using his own low pressure engines. One reasonably successful experiment was, however, conducted by the industrialist Patrick Miller who asked engineer Robert Symington to build him a paddle steamer, which was tried out at Loch Dalswinton in Dumfries. It was a very cumbersome device with a big, wide-cylindered engine driving two paddle-wheels which pushed the boat through the water at the unremarkable rate of two knots. Among those who turned out to view the venture was a local farmer, better known for his verse than agriculture, Robert Burns.

In 1800, Watt's patent expired and there was some rather more purposeful activity. Symington was again called in to build a paddle steamer. It was commissioned by the Secretary of State for War, Henry Dundas, who was also a governor of the Forth and Clyde Canal. In March 1802, the steam tug, *Charlotte Dundas*, pulled two seventy-ton barges down the canal for nineteen miles at the rate of just over three miles an hour, and that against a strong head wind. It was, in some ways, a highly successful experiment, but the canal proprietors decided the wash was damaging the banks, so that was the end of that. Other observers were, however, most impressed by what they saw. An American, Robert Fulton, started up his own paddle steamer, the *Clermont*, on the Hudson, between New York and Albany, so beginning the long and highly successful story of the American river steamers. Nearer home, river traders were less concerned with the evil effects of wash on their banks than the canal proprietors had been. A captured French privateer, *L'Actif*, was fitted out with a steam engine and began work in August 1813, after which, under her new name, the *Experiment*, she regularly ran along the River Yare between Yarmouth and Norwich. More important, as far as commercial development was concerned, was the introduction of regular steam tug services on both the Trent and the Severn by 1814. Steam had arrived on the water, but it was still only applied to paddle boats.

Between 1836 and 1838, two engineers were working independently on replacing paddle propulsion by the screw propeller. Francis Pettit Smith made a number of successful experiments with a steam launch, in the course of which he discovered that increasing the size of the propeller did not necessarily increase the speed of the vessel. In an accident half the launch's propeller was knocked off and to Smith's astonishment the speed of the vessel increased. The other experimenter was a Swede, John Ericsson, who in 1829 had achieved a measure of fame as designer of the locomotive *Novelty* which unsuccessfully competed against Stephenson's *Rocket* at the Rainhill Trials. He fitted a canal boat with a screw propeller and sent it on a trip round England from London to Manchester and back. It turned in average speeds of five to six m.p.h. on the canals and nine m.p.h. on the deeper waters of the rivers. These were excellent results—indeed, today Ericsson's boat would have been breaking the official speed limits! Unfortunately, canals and rivers were considered old hat, left-overs from the previous century. Railways were the thing and railway companies were actually buying up canals, not to improve them but to keep a check on competition. When, in 1856, a new steam tug, the *Pioneer*, was tried out by the Moira Colliery on the Ashby Canal, the railway company banned it on the old grounds of bank damage. But the *Pioneer* had two contra-rotating propellers which produced very little wash, and the colliery successfully won a Court action to allow them to use the boat.

By the mid-nineteenth century, however, the sight of a steam boat was by no means uncommon on the rivers of Britain. They came in a variety of shapes and sizes, with both paddle and screw propulsion. Many were no more than the old-style river boats with some of the cargo space sacrificed to make way for an engine. The narrow boats which travelled throughout the Midlands canal system and on the major rivers, Trent, Severn and Thames, were given engines by the carrying companies in an attempt to fight off the growing competition from the railways. The engines were particularly useful on the river sections, where the old horse often had trouble struggling against the strong current. One notorious danger spot was at the junction between the Trent and the Erewash Canal. There the horses had to be taken across the river by ferry, while the boats were hauled across by a winch. On one occasion, a pair of boats was being winched over when the cable snapped: one vessel ran aground on an island, while the second was swept up against the railway bridge, just above an unprotected weir. There it was tipped sideways by the current and its cargo slid into the water. A local poet wrote a parody of the song, *Sweet Afton*, renaming it, *Sweet Trent*: very apt, for the lost cargo was sugar, which promptly dissolved.

The most famous fleet of narrow boats was that belonging to Fellows, Morton and Clayton who introduced steam power in the 1880s. The company prided itself on running the smartest, cleanest and fastest service in the country. The brasswork and paintwork would have passed inspection by the most meticulous of Petty Officers, and there was even a curtain hung between the boiler and the engine to keep the latter free from dust. The crew had white overalls and white cord trousers—and woe betide any crew member whose clothes were not spotless. There were seven men working two boats: the motor boat in front, the engineless 'butty' behind. It may seem a large crew, but these were fly boats, working right round the clock. Working on F.M.C. boats was hard and demanding but the pay was good, and many a man put up with the endless work programme, hoping to earn enough to buy his own boat.

Different rivers developed their own characteristic craft, of which the most striking were undoubtedly the 'Tom Puddings', which traded on the Aire and Calder. These were boats at their simplest, just oblong iron boxes, fastened together to form a train, which could consist of anything up to 32 such boxes. As each of the containers was around 20 foot long by 16 foot beam, carrying 35 tons, they would have formed a snaking, flexible train, over 200 yards long with a load of over 1,000 tons. The first of these boxes had a pointed front to act as a dummy bows, and the truly remarkable fact is that at first it was customary for the steam tug to be at the back of the train. Wires ran along the side of the train to the dummy bows, so that the whole thing could be steered, though this can hardly have been an easy matter. Later the operators reverted to a more conventional arrangement with the tug at the front, and in that form they can be seen to this day on the waters of the Aire and Calder, taking coal from the South Yorkshire coalfield to the port of Goole. There the 'Tom Puddings' are picked up by a hydraulic lift and emptied into waiting colliers for their trip round the coast.

Traditionally, the busiest of all rivers as far as the coal trade is concerned had been the Tyne, serving the vast coalfields of the north-east. It was here, in 1852, that the very first screw collier, the *John Bowes*, began its working life. This steamer, built at Jarrow, could carry 650 tons and could do the round trip from Tyne to Thames in five days, where the old sailing coasters had taken a month. She was kept on in the Tyne until 1898, when she was sold off to Scandinavia and ended her days in Spain as the *Villa Selgas*. She met her end, still at work after nearly a century, when she foundered in a gale in 1933 and sank.

Screw propulsion had been shown very early on to have great advantages, particularly for ocean-going vessels, but the paddle steamer was by no means finished when the screw steamer came in. It had a long career on rivers throughout the country, proving particularly useful as a ferry. There were also 'market boats' which, as their name suggests, served the local markets, carrying produce, cattle and passengers. Such a boat used to run from Chepstow, down the Wye, across the Severn, into the Avon and up to Bristol. The original market boats were trows, but in 1826 a steamship, the *Wye*, was launched at Bristol, the first steamer to be built in the port which was later to see the ships of Isambard Kingdom Brunel take to the water. The *Wye* was no *Great Britain*, but she did just what her makers had hoped she would. The trows had taken two days for the return journey; the newcomer ran from Bristol to Chepstow in 1 hour 55 minutes 'highly to the satisfaction of several experimental engineers on board'. She was followed by an iron-hulled vessel in 1843, which offered a fast and comfortable service at the very modest charge of three shillings for a cabin (five shillings day return), while those who were content to stay on deck could travel for just half that sum. By 1861, the third *Wye* had cut the journey time to 1 hour 23 minutes. It was to be a short-lived triumph. In 1863, the Bristol and South West Railway opened, and the passengers deserted the steam packet for the new trains.

If any one river can be said to have special associations with the days of the paddle steamers, then that river is the Clyde. It had the honour to see the first-ever steam passenger service in Britain—just missing being the world's first, thanks to Fulton's efforts on the Hudson. However, it was in 1812 that Henry Bell, a hotel owner from Helensburgh, gave orders for John Wood of Port Glasgow to build a steamer. It was a tiny vessel, 45 foot overall, with a displacement of 2½ tons and, though her top speed was only around 6 knots, she was given the name *Comet*. If not as fast as a comet, she proved to be equally short-lived. After her completion in April 1812, she was set to work doing three trips a week between Glasgow and Greenock. The scheme was not a success, and for a while she worked the Firth of Forth, before being taken out of service in 1819, when she was fitted with new engines and had her length increased to 65½ feet. She worked briefly on the coastal route between Glasgow and Fort William, but sank in December 1820. The engine of this pioneer Clyde steamer was saved and is now in the Science Museum in London.

If *Comet* was not an unqualified success, the steamers that followed undoubtedly were. The Clyde is a river which undergoes remarkable changes in its character. At Glasgow, the river is surrounded by industry and the shipyards; but as you move out into the estuary, so the buildings and the bustle are left behind and the scenery is typical of the Highlands and the Islands, and that is the same as saying that it is among the finest scenery to be found anywhere in the world. So what better treat could there be for the citizens of cramped and crowded Glasgow than an excursion down their river on one of the big fleet of excursion cruisers? Happily, one can still relive something of those splendid days. The Clyde can no longer boast, as once it did, the largest excursion fleet in Britain, but it can boast the last of the great sea-going paddle steamers. The *Waverley* was built in 1947 for the London and North Eastern Railway, and though she is a twentieth-century craft and has the lines of a twentieth-century craft, she still has about her all the atmosphere of the previous century.

Steam boats came in as many varieties as had sail: tugs, barges, coasters and the larger sea-going vessels that made use of the river ports and harbours. But, as vessels grew ever larger, so the demands on ports increased. Old ports decayed, unable to cope, while new ports expanded to take their place. No port expanded faster than Liverpool, facing westward across the Atlantic and serving the thriving industrial community of the north-west. The expansion of the cotton industry that transformed the manufacturing towns also transformed the trade of the Mersey. There was cotton coming in from the Far East and America, finished goods going out to the world and by the end of the eighteenth century, there was that most profitable of all trades—slaves. At that time, it was estimated that a quarter of all vessels in Liverpool were slavers and this represented half the entire slave trade of Europe. It was strongly supported by local politicians who even issued verses, boasting of their backing for the trade at election times:

Be true to the man who stood true to his Trust,
Remember our sad situation we must;
When our African business was near at an end,
Remember, my lads, 'twas Gascoyne was our friend.

If our slave trade had gone, there's an end to our lives,
Beggars all we must be, our children and wives;
No ships from our ports their proud sails o'er would spread,
And our streets grown with grass, where the cows might be fed.

The end of the wretched trade did not, in fact, bring ruin to the Mersey. On the contrary, the port continued to grow, for traffic was increasing all the time. There were times, indeed, when it seemed that everything would end with the river just one solid, unmovable block of ships. Richard Ayton, who wrote a book describing a voyage round Great Britain in 1814, paints a memorable picture of Liverpool and the river a century and a half ago.

Liverpool was no longer a place where ships were simply to be seen riding at anchor in mid-river. It had proper wet docks, which could be closed off by lock gates to keep a constant water level, enabling ships to tie up to the quay for loading and unloading. When Ayton paid his visit, the docks covered around thirty-five acres, 'and the whole of this space is generally completely filled up by vessels, whose masts and rigging, confounded together, raise an idea of numbers even more considerable than really exist'. The dock was almost surrounded by shops and warehouses, 'far more vast than anything of the kind that the metropolis can boast'. The ships 'are frequently so jammed together, that they fill up a dock in one solid mass'.

The somewhat thankless task of attempting to control the movement into and out of the docks fell to the dock master. To succeed in that task demanded an organizing genius who deserved far more than the £105 a year which was all he was paid. Individual ships trying to thread their way through the massed hulls, were sometimes so damaged in the process that before they could put to sea they had to turn round and come back to dock again for repairs. That, however, was as nothing compared to the business of getting a whole fleet under way.

We had the luck to be present when two hundred sail, principally West Indiamen, were undocked in a single tide, and they made their way amidst such a confusion of obstacles, such a conflict of commands and opinions, such peals of swearing, such showers of blocks, snapping of ropes, and cracking of bowsprits and quarter-boards, that it was really astonishing to us, to see them, all in the course of an hour, all safe and afloat in the river.

A growing overseas trade with improved communications down rivers and canals brought enormous changes to many riverside industries. Goods which had previously been limited to a local market now found their way all over the country and beyond to foreign customers. So there were certainly some industries which could be said to depend on rivers in every possible way. And few were more dependent than those designed to meet the taste for the cup that cheers and inebriates. Take, for example, that noble fluid of Scotland, much praised by the national poet:

> Oh! Willie brew'd a peck o' maut,
> An Rob a' Allan cam' to pree;
> Three blyther hearts, that lee long night,
> Ye wed na find in Christendie.
> We are na fou, we're na that fou,
> But just a drappie in air e'e;
> The cock may craw, the day may daw,
> And eye we'll taste the Whasky o.

Whisky, whasky, usquabagh, the water of life—whatever name you give the liquor distilled from the malt has a long and honourable, if not always quite legal, history. In fact, in the eighteenth century, it was all but impossible to distil whisky and sell it and still keep within the law. It was, however, an attractively profitable trade. A recipe for 1729, for 'fine usquebagh' lists some unlikely ingredients, but shows a remarkable profitability:

	£	s	d
5 gallons of proof Molasses spirits at 2s 7½d	00	13	01½
6 gallons of proof rectify'd malt spirts at 20d	00	10	00
Mace and cloves each one ounce and a half	00	03	09
Nutts 4 ounces and a half	00	05	01½
Cinnamon 3 ounces			
Coriander seed, Ginger, each 3 ounces	00	00	03
Cubebs 1 ounce and a half	00	00	04½
Raisins 4 pounds ½	00	01	06

Dates 3 pounds	00	04	00
Liquorice 2 pounds ¼	00	01	06
Best English saffron 4 ounces and a half	00	11	03
10 pounds Lisbon Sugar at 7d½	00	06	03
	02	17	01½

This little lot produced ten pounds worth of whisky for an expenditure of less than three pounds. No wonder then that the Scots proved enthusiastic and very expert manufacturers of moonshine hooch. It became a battle between the excise men on one side and not just the distillers, but often the whole community, on the other. It was easy enough to hide a still, but very difficult to get rid of the tell-tale smoke. One excise man trailed a suspicious character heading off into the woods with a sack of grain. It was night time and to the official's great mystification, he found himself following a horse and a sack of grain one minute and horse minus sack the next. The grain, it seemed, had vanished. He went back the next day and there, hidden under boulders, he found a trapdoor leading to a cave and the illicit still. And the smoke? Well, that was led away down a long flue to emerge eventually at the bottom of the distiller's own chimney at home. The Scots were masters of the distiller's art, only matched in enthusiasm by the Irish. There, no fewer than 19,007 illicit stills were actually smashed between 1811 and 1813, and no one had any notion of how many remained undetected. The authorities estimated that four million gallons of poteen were sold every year, but they had to admit that the figure was only a guess. As any visitor to the west coast of Ireland will tell you, they are still at it—and very palatable the best poteen is too, once you have got over the initial shock to the system.

In 1825, the Chancellor brought in a law establishing rectifiers between the makers of spirit from grain and the drinking public. Now decent whisky could be openly made and openly sold, and the Scots knew after their years in hiding just which rivers to go to for the water for the brew. The Scottish distilleries were on their way to fame and fortune. In 1889, a gentleman by the name of Alfred Barnard produced a guide to the whisky distilleries of the United Kingdom. 'Having long been possessed with an ardent desire to see the Distilleries of Scotland and Ireland, I took the first opportunity that presented itself,' he wrote in his introduction. 'And,' he continued, 'knowing the task set before me would occupy at least two years, made arrangements to transfer my duties to others.' In those two years, he was to visit 161 distilleries, 129 of them in Scotland. There was no shortage of volunteers ready to help him with his work, though no one kept a note of their condition at the end of the trip.

The first stage in producing whisky is to steep the barley in pure water from a nearby river or stream—and the quality of that water will have a profound effect on the flavour of the final drink. At just the right moment in the germination process, the barley is taken away to be dried over the peat fires of the kiln and the peat, like the water, imparts its own distinctive flavour. The barley is now known as malt. The malt is crushed and thoroughly mixed with water before yeast is added for fermentation. After that the liquor is removed to the giant copper to be double distilled before casking up in oak barrels to mature. Geography has an important part to play in the quality of the whisky, and certain rivers were found to be ideal. Among these, the Spey stands supreme. Barnard went to Speyside and rhapsodized over the scenery: 'How the road winds! What hills we ascend and descend, what peeps amid the trees of the tortuous course of the beautiful stream. . . . Gazing from this Eden-like valley to the horizon, we see, on all sides, picturesque outsteppings of mountains and hills.' But the best was yet to come. 'We ascended an eminence from which can be seen, almost in a circle, no less than seven distilleries!' All this, helped no doubt by the dram which inevitably accompanied each visit, led Barnard on to new lyrical heights. 'In this retired spot, far removed from noisy cities and prying eyes, surrounded by all that is beautiful and lovely in nature, is carried on the mystery of John Barleycorn,—his death, burial and resurrection. No wonder with these surroundings that the pure spirit emerging from such an Eden should be appreciated by mortals all the world over.'

In Barnard's day, the scene was peaceful. In the past, though, there had been bloody battles between moonshiners and excise men, and those who came to establish legal stills in the 1820s had to face the anger of the old smugglers. When the Smith family established the famous Glenlivet distillery at Speyside, the founder always went about armed. But those days passed, and the little port of Lossiemouth was kept busy sending out the water of life to a grateful world.

Barnard declared himself encouraged by the success of his distillery guide and decided that he could, after all, spare another two years from business. He turned from the great national drink of Scotland to that of England. There had been, for many generations, those who opposed such foreign habits as drinking spirits, as this popular Elizabethan verse makes clear:

All fiery spirits damn'd, I need not tell,
The more we drink, the more's the flame in hell;
Drink beer, to us by nature giv'n,
When so inclined you'll find the way to heaven.

The arts of the brewer and the distiller are not that different, both starting with malted barley which is mashed with water to convert the grain's starch into sugar. But in brewing, the process of turning sugar into alcohol by fermentation is not continued into the later strengthening process of distillation. And other ingredients are added, notably hops, which act both as a preservative and a flavouring agent. Water for brewing also has to possess the right qualities, which is why the great centres of the brewing industry developed at Burton-on-Trent. Not that river water was itself used in the process: the great attraction was in the local springs. But the river was to have a vital role in the expansion of the industry.

In the eighteenth century, there were some fifteen types of beer brewed in the area, ranging from porter, brown stout and the very rich Welch Ale to the delicate London Ale, table beer for the family, special beer for haymakers and the particularly nasty-sounding Scurvy-Grass Ale, described as 'a great purifier of the blood'. You can still find *that* around lurking under some deceptively innocuous trade names. There were famous names even then but, as the anonymous eighteenth-century poet celebrating the worth of Allsop's declared:

> Such ale as this, wherever sought,
> None other could invent sirs!
> 'Tis only brewed, 'tis only bought,
> At Burton-upon-Trent, sirs.

Changes in brewing began with the opening of the Trent Navigation and the Trent and Mersey Canal in the eighteenth century. These changes can be traced in the story of one of Burton's favourite sons, Bass. The company was founded in the eighteenth century, and for a time did a busy trade with Eastern Europe and the Baltic States. Where only 740 barrels had been sent overseas from Hull in 1750, over 11,000 barrels were exported in 1780. Then, as is the way with export trades, political upheavals in Europe brought a temporary halt. The head of the company, Michael Thomas Bass, set out to look for new markets.

The answer was found in the British Empire on which the sun never sets, and as the sun is a great bringer of thirsts, Bass set out to slake the thirsts of British India. He brewed a light, sparkling ale which he called East India

Pale Ale. Later, the 'East' was dropped from the name, and eventually it was shortened to its now familiar initials, I.P.A. Now the Trent was again busy with trade from the breweries, and it was to become even busier, thanks to what seemed at the time to be a catastrophe. In 1827, a ship bound for Calcutta with 300 casks of I.P.A. was wrecked in the Irish Sea. The casks themselves were salvaged unharmed and were eventually auctioned off at Liverpool. The locals tasted I.P.A. for the first time and found they liked it. The drink brewed for the lonely administrator in the Himalayas was now in demand throughout Britain. When Barnard visited Bass in the 1880s, the brewery covered 145 acres, served by twelve miles of railway along which the company ran their own train. They also owned thirty-seven maltings.

Burton was not the only brewing centre in the land. London and other major cities all had several breweries, and there was even a 'Burton of the North' at Tadcaster. It was a good place for business. There was even a local trade right on the doorstop, for Tadcaster stood on the main London to Edinburgh coach road, and up to seventy coaches a day, each full of thirsty passengers, called in at the Angel Hotel. Like Burton, it owed much of its prosperity to its situation on a navigable river, the Wharfe, which connected with the Aire and Calder to the south. The most famous brewery was that of John Smith, who took over an older company in 1847, and he in turn passed it on to the even more enterprising William Smith in 1879. The latter decided to invest in a new, wholly modern brewery, no expense spared. It was, as Barnard discovered, an impressive sight. 'From the railway, we could but observe that the dull old town, with its few gas lamps, looked dismal and lonesome, in striking contrast to the brewery, which appeared so radiant in the surrounding darkness.'

He also noted that production had risen from 500 barrels a week in the 1870s to 3,000 barrels in the '80s. So the beer of John Smith continued to find favour for the last part of the century, before it finally fell to one of the big companies of the present day. Some of the great beers are still with us, and some were even praised in verse by the poet, C. S. Calverley:

> O Beer! O Hodgson, Guinness, Allsopp, Bass!
> Names that should be on every infant's tongue!
> Shall days and months and years and centuries pass,
> And still your merits go unrecked, unsung?
> Oh! I have gazed into my foaming glass,
> And wished that lyre could again be strung
> Which once rang prophet-like through Greece and taught her
> Misguided sons that the best drink is water.

The breweries used, and use, huge quantities of water in their process, but the finished brew is no longer carried away in boats. Even in Barnard's day the railways had taken a lot of the trade away from the river. And what was true of brewing was equally true of other industries. Road and railway were both competing with the rivers for trade, and in that competition the rivals were constantly on the look-out for ways of improving their own system. The river navigation companies were bitter opponents of the new railways, but just as they had lost out in their attempt to stop the spread of canals, so now they lost out to the railways. And there were constant reminders of the ignominy of the loss of trade to both road and rail traffic in the new generation of bridges thrown across the rivers by the new generation of engineers.

If the eighteenth century was the great age of the stone bridge, then unquestionably the nineteenth century was the great age of iron and steel, though the most famous successor to the tradition of Rennie and Telford started his career in river crossing by going under rather than over the water. In 1825, after numerous false starts, work was begun on building a tunnel under the Thames. The company chairman performed the inauguration ceremony. The chief engineer, Marc Brunel, laid the first brick of the excavation shaft, while the second brick was laid by his son, Isambard Kingdom Brunel.

The tunnel under the Thames from Rotherhithe to Wapping was very much a triumph for the father, but one that was hard won. Geology was a science in its infancy, yet the geologists came up with absolutely confident predictions of the nature of the ground out of sight beneath the water. It was, they declared, solid clay all the way. They were completely wrong. Far from being solid anything, it was often loose, shifting gravel. Yet in spite of this the work went forward—and might well have gone forward in safety had the financial backers been prepared to listen to their chief engineer. They were seduced away by the siren song of profit.

Brunel devised a shield consisting of twelve cast-iron frames, six frames to each of the tunnel's arches, and three storeys to each frame. This structure formed the protection for the workmen in the thirty-six compartments, who had the job of excavating the face in front of them. Whilst working, they were completely protected, but as excavation continued, so the shield had to be moved forward by jacks. The heavy, wooden protecting boards had to be taken out and replaced, so for a time the tunnel was quite unprotected. Marc Brunel treated this move with extreme caution. He allowed for a forward movement of only four-and-a-half inches at a time. The company became dissatisfied with this rate of progress. From the safety of their offices, they decreed the forward movement should be doubled, and then compounded the danger by taking the men off day rates and putting them on piece work. The workers were to be rewarded for speed not safety. Marc Brunel was a worried man. To add to his anxieties, the company was letting visitors down to see the amazing new technological miracle.

Marc Brunel's diary for May 1827 records his disquiet. On the thirteenth, he wrote that 'the whole of the ground over our heads must have been in movement, and that, too, at high water. The shield must, therefore, have supported upwards of six hundred tons! It has walked many weeks with that weight twice a day, over its head! Notwithstanding every prudence on our part a disaster may still occur.' It did, six nights later. As the shield was being moved, the roof collapsed and a flood of water broke through into the tunnel. The men fled before the torrent, rushing for the spiral staircase that led up the shaft to safety. When it seemed that all was safe, a cry was heard from the darkness. Isambard Brunel at once grabbed a rope and shinned down an iron stanchion towards the blackness of the rising water. He re-emerged with Tillett, an elderly man who was in charge of the pumping engine. Miraculously, Brunel had found him and pulled him out of the water. Even more miraculously, when numbers were counted, it was found that not a single life had been lost in the flood.

The disaster did not mean the end of work in the tunnel, though it was a long and dangerous job clearing the workings. At last, everything was back in order and Brunel celebrated the event with a brilliant piece of showmanship. To demonstrate his confidence, he held a banquet in the tunnel on 10 November. Such confidence was, however, short-lived, and as work restarted he again began to fear flooding. It came on 12 January. The water again burst through. The assistant engineer, Richard Beamish, hearing the cries of panic, broke open the door at the foot of the stairway used by visitors and found, borne to him on the flood, the seemingly lifeless body of Isambard Brunel. Brunel recovered, but six workmen lost their lives. Work on the tunnel was stopped for seven years. It eventually restarted in 1835, but it was 1843 before the great work was finally completed and Marc Brunel, now in his seventies, could enjoy his triumph. He also received a knighthood: few have done more to deserve such an honour—and a good many considerably less. His tunnel is still in use, but now carries tube trains between Rotherhithe and Wapping.

Isambard Brunel was already busy with other matters by the time work on the tunnel was completed, and had acquired an even greater reputation than his father. He, too, was actively concerned with river crossings, but by bridge rather than by tunnel. Of his road bridges, the most famous and certainly the most spectacular was the bridge across the Avon at Clifton. The progress of work on building a bridge across the Avon gorge made that on the Thames tunnel seem almost indecently rapid. It all started in 1753, when a Bristolian wine merchant, William Vick, left a legacy of £1,000 which was to be invested until interest accumulated to raise it to £10,000 at which point, he hoped, it would pay for a bridge. Forty years later, with funds still crawling up towards the magic £10,000, the first design appeared. It was by the appropriately named William Bridges, though nothing else was appropriate about the design, which resembled a multi-storey block of flats, filling the gorge, with an arch in the middle for ships. No one took that very seriously.

In 1829, the funds had reached £8,000 and the trustees decided time had arrived for serious planning. A Bridge Company was formed, and it was decided to hold a competition to find the best design. The most attractive and interesting design was Brunel's, but the organizing committee were, not surprisingly, somewhat chary about committing themselves and their cash to the care of a twenty-four-year-old. So they called in the Grand Old Man of British engineering, Thomas Telford, to give his opinion. Quite unsuitable, declared Telford. On being shown the rest, he declared them equally unsuitable. Would Mr Telford consider submitting his own design? Mr Telford would and did. It was an extraordinary piece of work, a suspension bridge, but one in which the piers were not, as in Brunel's design, at the top of the gorge, but at the bottom. These colossal structures were in the Gothic style, so that they resembled cathedral spires. The committee accepted the design, but public opinion was firmly against it. The old designs were brought out again, and the young Brunel's design was accepted. It was a wise move, for the result is one of the world's great bridges. But, as with so many engineering projects, the gap between planning and execution can prove more difficult to span than the river itself. In the case of Clifton Bridge, the constant interruptions caused chiefly by lack of cash—Mr Vick's £10,000 was soon spent—meant that the bridge was not finished in Brunel's lifetime. It was finally declared officially open on 8 December 1864.

The Clifton Bridge was by no means the first suspension bridge across a British river. Captain Robert Brown of the Royal Navy patented a method of making chain cable from wrought iron, and he used these for the Union Bridge across the Tweed near Berwick. This still survives as the oldest suspension bridge, but it cannot match the magnificence of Clifton. To be fair to Brown and his pioneering design, nature was very much on the side of Brunel. No one could ask for a grander and more beautiful setting, and in July 1970 it was the scene for an event which must have brought joy to Brunel as he looked down from whatever cloud is reserved for the best engineers. His pioneering ship, the *Great Britain*, was brought home to Bristol, passing on its way beneath the great bridge.

Brunel's name is associated less with roads than with railways, and it was the new generation of railway bridges that dominated the river scene of the nineteenth century. The river navigation authorities literally fought against the coming of the railways. They tried to prevent the surveyors for the first true mainline railway, the Liverpool and Manchester, going about their work at all. Captain Bradshaw of the Bridgewater Canal even went so far as to have guns fire at random over his land at night to stop the surveyors sneaking up in the dark. It was hopeless. The railways came and the owners of the Sankey Navigation had to look up at George Stephenson's new viaduct crossing the old waterway. Brunel himself was early on the scene with some splendid bridges for the Great Western Railway, including the brick bridge across the Thames near Maidenhead, which could boast the widest brick arches in the world. His finest effort was the Royal Albert Bridge across the Tamar at Saltash. It was his final triumph. He was a dying man when he was taken to see the finished work, drawn slowly across on a flat truck behind one of the GWR locomotives.

There are many magnificent railway bridges across Britain's rivers, especially in Scotland, starting at the border with the crossing of the Tweed and culminating in the huge cantilevered arches of the Forth bridge. They are so numerous and so magnificent that it is easy to think of the whole period as one in which triumph followed triumph in steady procession. One tends to forget the disasters. In 1878, the North British Railway opened the world's longest bridge across the River Tay. It was, declared William McGonagall, perhaps the most popular bad poet of all times, a magnificent sight:

> And ought to cheer the hearts of the passengers night and day
> As they are conveyed along the beautiful railway,
> And towering above the silvery Tay,
> Spanning the beautiful river shore to shore
> Upwards of two miles and more.

A year and a half after the opening, McGonagall was penning *The Great Tay Bridge Disaster*. The bridge blew down and a loaded passenger train dropped into the Firth. It was by no means the only railway bridge to collapse. One of the most picturesque of viaducts, which crosses the Nidd at Knaresborough, had a predecessor which collapsed, damming the river and causing extensive flooding. The only benefit the local citizens derived came from picking up fish from their front doorsteps.

The big railway viaducts dominated many a river valley, often forming a new focal point in an old scene. But the railways had another, far more profound, effect. As their trade grew, so the trade of many rivers declined. This had little effect on the deep, wide rivers serving major ports, but for inland waterways the effect could be disastrous. There were obvious immediate casualties. As the new viaducts opened over the Forth, Tay, or Wye, so the old ferries began to close, and many of the bulk goods that had gone by barge were sent by goods train. Not that life went from the rivers: some were busier than ever but with a very different type of traffic. The Thames, in particular, was crowded with boats as the railways brought the boaters out of the city to enjoy a day, a weekend, or even a week on the river.

> Here, then, behold our day begun,
> The early train is starting,
> And unromantic Paddington
> Frowns down on our departing.
> And soon we breathe an ampler air
> As, through the suburbs stealing
> We run past Act-on (always 'square')
> And say goodbye to Ealing . . .
> . . . Taplow gravel-pits hail in sight,
> And look! where the sunbeams quiver,
> There, so beautiful, brave and bright,
> Is our well-beloved river!

The lines come from an anonymous poem, *A River Holiday*, published in 1883. The river trip was a major outing organized with care. Everyone dressed up for the occasion: the men in flannels, boaters and alarmingly striped blazers, the girls in lightweight frocks with parasols. It was a reversal of the Victorian norm, with the men displaying the brighter plumage and, like all courting birds, they strutted and displayed and showed off their prowess. The popular spots, such as Boulter's Lock, were a mass of skiffs, punts and launches, each with its full complement of these brightly coloured species. The highlight of the day was the picnic on the bank—and that was more than a squashed sandwich and a thermos of tepid tea. *A River Holiday* again:

> Two or three dozens of plovers' eggs,
> Some ducklings plump and tender;
> Give the girls the wings, distribute the legs
> Amongst the masculine gender!
> A toothful of punch à la Romaine,
> (Slice the cucumber, Freddy—)
> Cool the Burgundy and Champagne
> In the stream until we're ready.
> Strawberries? Cream? No, not just now,
> They will do a trifle later;
> Tom, bring the ices, there in the bow,
> From our little refrigerator.

Heaven knows how they managed to row back after that lot. Over the years, one account of the Thames holiday has retained its popularity, Jerome K. Jerome's *Three Men in a Boat*. Some dislike its mixture of broad humour and sentimentality, rambling narrative and romanticized history but, in his best moments, Jerome catches the special appeal of the river as few others have done. He also had some choice words to say on the subject of other river users, such as the anglers. His view of the sport on the Thames suggests that he himself was enthusiastic, but not perhaps especially skilful:

> The neighbourhood of Streatley and Goring is a great fishing centre. There is some excellent fishing. . . . The local fisherman's guide doesn't say a word about catching anything. All it says is 'a good station for fishing'; and from what I have seen of the district, I am quite prepared to bear out this statement. There is no spot in the world where you can get more fishing, or where you can fish for a longer period. . . . You can hang on and fish for a year, if you want to, it will all be the same.

Jerome's fishermen, it seems, never catch anything, but are, without exception, masters of the art of fiction. The amount of space he devotes to descriptions of the sport is a measure of its popularity in Victorian times. It was the age of the riparian landlord, and the huntin', shootin' and fishin' brigade, who also pursued other river sports, such as otter hunting. It was also the age when fishing spread from the privileged classes to become a truly popular pastime. The age that rediscovered the writings of Izaak Walton produced its own literature in imitation of his style. Between 1821 and 1832, a series of anonymous poems was published in Newcastle, under the title,

The Fisher's Garland. No one would pretend that they are literary master-
pieces, but they often have a wonderful freshness and enthusiasm about
them. The authors are in love with their subject, and write directly from
experience. They can capture the delight of fishing in a way that can surpass
their master. Here is part of *The Old Fisher's Challenge*:

> O! Let it be in April-tide,
> But one of April's best,
> A mornin' that seems made o' May,
> In dews an' sunshine drest;
> Frae off the Crags o' Simonside
> Let the fresh breezes blow,
> And let old Cheviot's sides be green,
> Albeit his head be snow.
>
> Let the stream glitter i' the sun;
> The curl be on the pool,
> The rash gale ruffin' aye its face
> Aneath the Alders cool;
> Or if the Spring will have her clouds,
> Then let them pass me soon;
> Or if they have a thought and stay,
> Then let it be at noon.
>
> O! freshly from his mountain holds
> Comes down the rapid Tyne;—
> But Coquet's still the stream o' streams,
> So let her still be mine;
> There's many a sawmon lies in Tweed
> And many a trout in Till;
> But Coquet—Coquet aye for me,
> If I may have my will.

Substitute one's own favourite river for Coquet and one has every angler's
prayer; an expression of delight not just in the joys of fishing, but in the
pleasures of scenery, in good weather shared with good friends. As another
robust verse puts it:

> Then luck be to the Angler Lads,
> Luck to the rod and line;
> Wi' morn's first beam we'll wade the stream,
> The night we'll wet wi' wine.

Looking back at the years before the First World War, one does not think
primarily of fishing, nor even of declining commercial trade, great bridges

and industrial development. Mention rivers and Edwardian Britain, and the first image that springs to mind is of the pleasure boats, of the crowded Thames lock with rowing skiff and steam launch, of the Clyde steamers with the happy holiday crowds lining the rails. Yet no soothsayer at the beginning of the century would, one feels, have seen the changes nor guessed how rapidly they would come about. The twentieth century has also seen its changes and there seems to be every possibility that there are still more to come. Will there be dramatic changes? Will they come about with the speed that they did in the nineteenth century? Such questions lead to some interesting speculations.

CHAPTER SEVEN

Towards the future

Trying to assess where we stand today in our relationship with the veins in the national body is by no means simple. Looked at from some points of view, our interest in the rivers that thread the land has diminished: on a straightforward head count of installations using river water, we are doing less well now than we were when Domesday Book was compiled more than nine centuries ago. The rivers are no longer a major source of power, they no longer provide a major transport route for industry, nor do they make a substantial contribution to the nation's food supply. One might think that wherever one looked, the role of the river had diminished. Happily, that is not altogether true.

River traffic has diminished quite rapidly in the twentieth century: what the railways had begun, the motor lorry concluded. The old equation showing movement overland as being several times more expensive than movement by water still held good, but transport users were prepared to pay the price. The lorry could go, literally, from door to door. There was no trans-shipment, no waiting around at quaysides. It was worth paying to ensure quick delivery. Throughout this century, we have watched as commercial traffic on the roads has grown and grown, while that on the rivers has declined. Many once busy navigations fell into total disuse: locks decayed, wharves crumbled. Even the busiest rivers felt the effects: and just as river traffic decayed, so too did the river ports, even the mightiest of them.

Road traffic put an end to trade at many inland ports: increased size of ships and new handling methods had their effect on the seaports based beside the major rivers. The old linear ports with no proper harbour protection had already gone, but, as the twentieth century advanced, so the modernized ports, with their great acreage of enclosed docks, began to suffer in their turn, in spite of efforts at improvement. Work on the Tyne had only begun in the 1850s, with the establishment of the Tyne Improvement

Commission. They began by building two vast piers to protect the river from the sea and in 1861 a comprehensive improvement plan was drawn up by the Commissioners' engineer, J. F. Ure, which involved widening, deepening and straightening fourteen miles of the river so that it could be used by the biggest ships afloat. Then, in the 1900s, the Commissioners were given further powers to dredge nineteen miles of river to an unlimited depth. The old days of the narrow, meandering, frequently silted Tyne were over: the new, deep, straight river had arrived. The Commissioners could now proudly claim to have done their work and done it well. On 22 April 1907, the SS *Mauretania*, then the largest vessel in the world at 790 foot length, left the shipyard of Swan, Hunter and Wigham Richardson to pass down the river and out into the sea. She had a draught of 32 foot 6 inches. To ensure the depth of water to float such large craft, the Commissioners estimated that by the end of 1924 they had dredged slightly over 149 million tons of material. As a result, the official Tyne Handbook for 1925 could announce a total of 11,173 vessels using the port, representing a total tonnage of over 11 million tons. And the list of foreign ports reached by regular steamer services from Newcastle ranged from Aalborg to Vancouver. It was the age of great ships: cargo ships and passenger ships, built on the Clyde or the Tyne, plied the oceans of the world. The ports that served them grew as well—Hull, Glasgow and, most dramatically, Liverpool. The wet docks spread along more and more of the waterfront until, by the mid-twentieth century, they covered seven miles of river bank. Even as late as the 1950s one could still catch a passenger boat to cross the Atlantic, though even the Cunarders were dwarfed by the massive cranes and warehouses. And, of course, there was always the Port of London, still the biggest of them all.

Just when it must have seemed that trade might go on growing for ever, and the ports with it, the decline set in. The great depression hit ship-building especially hard and, in the postwar years, competition appeared. Just as the motor lorry hit inland water trade, now the aeroplane appeared as a new threat to maritime traffic. The passenger liners were simply obliterated from the scene. Why spend days on a ship when you can do the same journey in hours by air? Those of us lucky enough to have tried the old method could supply a few answers. Arriving at Liverpool, one simply sauntered through Customs, wandered up the gang-plank and there you were: the journey had begun. Sitting down to a splendid meal, one could look at the Liver Building, with its famous birds, as the ship slid out on to the tide—with considerably more ease than the sailing boats of a century before.

It was a relaxing and civilized way to travel, compared with the hustle of the airport, the interminable waits in dreary lounges, the packed seating and plastic meals of the jumbo jet. But it was undeniably expensive and time-consuming. Now it has all gone: no more liners make their way up the Mersey. The new has its undoubted advantages, but one cannot help mourning the passing of the old.

The motor lorry was soon recognized as a threat to inland shipping, but it was not so obvious that it would also have an effect on the big river ports. The lorry offered a fast service, but it was eventually realized that a good deal of time was being lost loading it up with a variety of oddly shaped objects and different-sized packing cases. The answer was the container—a standardized giant packing case to fit standardized trucks at both ends of a journey, with a standardized container ship in between. Now all that was needed for a truly efficient system was a standardized method of handling at the port—and a new generation of ports designed specifically for the container ship began to emerge. And that was not the end of the changes brought in by the shift to road transport. Cars and trucks run on oil and its derivative, petrol. In balmy, far-off days oil was a very cheap fuel. Everything, it seemed, could be run on oil. You could heat your home with it, either directly or indirectly—by using an oil burner yourself or waiting for the power stations to burn the oil to make electricity for you. And there was no shortage of other oil users in the vast petro-chemical industry. As the use of oil increased, so the use of coal decreased. The coal staithes that had lined the banks of Tyne, Tees and Wear fell into disuse, and there was no chance that they would be replaced by oil storage tanks. As the demand for the oil grew, so the vessels carrying it grew as well. The era of the supertanker had arrived and new deep-water ports developed with their accompanying storage tanks and refineries. Bristol declined—Avonmouth grew. No one had any use, it seemed, for the riverside marvels of the nineteenth century. Even the great London docks suffered. One of the first of the new generation of closed docks was St Katharine's, built by Telford. It was soon followed by its later and mightier neighbours. If you arrived at a prediction of what the commercial future would be by simply extending current trends, then it would seem that before long there will be no commercial traffic of any sort on Britain's rivers.

The future then might look bleak, but that old cost equation still stands. Water transport is cheaper than air, road or even rail, and economists have been forced to look to their sums as fuel costs go higher and higher. Whether there will be a revival in river transport or not remains to be seen. The case may be good, but there are imponderables, not the least of which is the thinking of politicians. It is unfortunate, in a way, that rivers were so successful in the past. It becomes too easy to argue that they were all right in their time but barges have as much relevance to modern transport as the pack-horse, while inland ports have outlived their usefulness. Anyone arguing for increased use of rivers is simply a romantic simpleton. If that is the case, then there are a great many romantic simpletons to be found across the channel where river navigation improvement has been a major feature of transport development.

In Europe, the rivers are busy with traffic, much of it in the shape of the peniche, the characteristic cargo barge of the rivers and canals. Peniches and other motorized barges, some with a displacement of well over a thousand tonnes, pass by with what seems to a British observer a quite astonishing regularity. They chug along, their blunt bows sending deep waves to the banks and many of them sport a Deux Chevaux or baby Fiat on deck for the captain when he ties up at the end of the day. It is possible to argue that all this busy traffic occurs simply because the rivers of France, Belgium, Germany and Holland are better suited to such trade than our native waterways: so they are, but only because authorities have taken the trouble to make them that way. New automatic locks have been built and new engineering marvels produced. Typical of the new thinking is the Ronquières inclined plane on the Brussels–Charleroi Canal in Belgium. At one time, boats went up and down the hillside by means of a flight of seventeen locks. Now that time-consuming process is in the past. Barges of up to 1,350 tonnes are floated into caissons—watertight containers like overgrown bath tubs. Each caisson has 236 wheels which run on a railed track and the whole tub, complete with its floating barge, is winched up the hillside. It covers a distance of nearly a mile during which it rises around 200 feet. At the top of the incline the barge is released to float out on to the upper level of the canal just twenty-two minutes after it came in at the bottom of the slope. Britain had inclined planes as early as the eighteenth century, but none survives in working form except as a museum piece. Obviously the cash investment in a device such as the Ronquières incline is enormous, but so it seems are the rewards. And as fuel prices escalate, so those rewards can only become greater. Is there any sign that Britain is willing to make a similar investment in her own system of river navigations?

Europe makes extensive use of inland water transport. Britain is now part of the European Community, therefore Britain should join in the system.

That plausible argument gained some ground in the 1970s. A number of ideas were brought forward for enabling the same barges to carry goods on both sides of the Channel without the bother and expense of trans-shipment. The two principal schemes were called LASH and BACAT, initials which stand for Lighter Aboard Ship and Barge Aboard Catamaran. Both schemes involved barges being loaded, rather like oversized containers, on to a mother ship for the Channel crossing, then being unloaded to continue inland by river and canal. The BACAT system, which involves barges being carried both on the deck of the mother ship and floating between its twin hulls, was actually introduced. The idea is immensely appealing. Goods from the steel-making district of Rotheram, for example, could be loaded on to a barge and would not then need to be unloaded until the barge reached its destination in the centre of Europe. The system went into operation—and failed; not because it was a badly thought-out scheme nor even because the economics turned out wrong. The stumbling block was the British docker. Trade at the traditional port of Hull was declining, and the dockers, alarmed at the prospect of being by-passed, blocked the scheme. The port was blockaded and BACAT died. There is little point now in speculating whether a different result might have been obtained by more careful planning and wider discussion. It happened and the scheme, for the present at least, is dead.

Other signs are slightly more hopeful. The 1980s have begun with a major scheme for the improvement of the Sheffield and South Yorkshire Navigation, which involves replacement of the old locks on the River Don. The improvement was much needed. European visitors, accustomed to their own highly efficient, fully automated systems, would be astounded at the sight of one solitary lock-keeper working all the machinery by hand. To add to the problem, the commercial boats normally found on that waterway travel in a train of three barges pulled by a tug. Only one barge can be fitted into the lock at a time, so the train has to be broken up and manhandled through. Small wonder, given such conditions, that few companies are prepared to think of the waterways as anything other than antiquated left-overs from the Industrial Revolution. Now, at least, a start has been made, though there is still no sign of investment in ambitious new schemes on the European model. Rising fuel costs and vanishing oil supplies may yet force the issue, at which point schemes will no doubt be started that will cost several times what they would have done had they been started now.

The commercial life of the rivers today is not limited to transport. Rivers provide a useful source of water for industry, and especially for power stations. A journey down the Trent, for example, is punctuated by cooling towers and at one particular spot, Trent Port—a grandiose name for what appears to be little more than a solitary landing stage—there are three power stations all in sight. Some might consider this at best a dubious blessing, but for those of us who actually like the elegant shape of the cooling towers, Trent Port is really rather special. To some extent, the power station and the river have retained something of the old working relationship, particularly with the coal-fired stations. There is clearly a great advantage to be gained from bringing in the fuel by water. On the Aire and Calder an ambitious scheme was begun to bring coal to Ferrybridge 'C' Power Station, and in 1966 the service was begun with push tugs shoving trains of three 160-tonne barges up the wharf. There they were plucked out of the water by a tippler and emptied into the storage containers. The idea was good—but the tippler was never very successful in practice.

The power stations, however, mostly look to the rivers beside them as overgrown water mains which are useful, even essential, but not part of the primary job of turning a generator to make electricity. But what are the chances of using the water itself as a power source? The water wheel has been around for a long time, and has been used, on a small scale, to generate electricity. Its big brother, the turbine, has been powered by the controlled flow of river water contained behind a dam, the latter-day equivalent of the mill pond. One old type of mill offers an interesting model for a new type of power producer. The tide mills used the rising estuary water by storing it behind a barrier at high tide and releasing it at low tide. Now, that is a method which looks as if it might have applications in the modern world—a reservoir that can be constructed without using up thousands of acres of valuable land.

Various schemes have been put forward for using wave power directly, and these might prove useful in the energy-starved twenty-first century, but for the immediate future schemes based on the tide mill principle look a better bet. Indeed, such a scheme has already been put into operation, but not in Britain. The installation was built across the River Rance in Brittany. A barrier, half a mile long, was constructed across the estuary, housing twenty-four turbines. These work both on the rising tide and on the ebb, but the system is not an unqualified success. It contributes no more than one per cent of France's power output. It has to be remembered, however, that this is a pioneering scheme and, like all such schemes, it has helped to point up the difficulties which will, one hopes, be solved in its successors. The actual design work goes back to 1938, though work was not begun until 1961. It has already taught us a lot, and the experience of the Rance barrage has helped British engineers in working out their plans.

The most likely site for the first British tidal barrage is the Severn estuary. The idea for a Severn barrage as a source of power goes back even further than the Rance. The first plans were drawn up in 1849, though it was not then thought of as part of an electricity generating scheme. Things have not progressed very much since. We still have no more than plans on paper. As with river improvements, there is a strong feeling around that events will conspire to ensure that plans will eventually be realized. The question that still has to be answered is how much foresight and daring will be shown by those in authority. At least, thanks to some studies in recent years, there is a basis on which one can build. We know the different forms such a scheme might take, and we know something of the likely returns. Estimates of cost are also available, but as estimates for major civil engineering works usually end up being wrong by several hundred per cent, one can be forgiven for not spending too much time on those particular statistics.

In 1978 and 1979 an ad hoc working party, under the auspices of the Advisory Council on Research and Development for Fuel and Power, prepared a study on the various tidal power schemes, concentrating mainly on the Severn barrage. Their recommendations were cautious and carefully phrased. It certainly seemed that if tidal power was to be used at all in Britain, then the Severn estuary was quite the best place. It is sufficiently narrow to ensure a good difference of levels between high and low tide, yet still large enough to provide a suitable volume of water. There are still many questions to be answered. One of the great difficulties with any scheme of this sort lies in the time difference between supply and demand. Demand for electricity varies throughout the day, with a well-defined pattern of peaks and troughs. Tides also vary throughout the day, but sadly it is only rarely that maximum tidal flow coincides with maximum demand for power. There are two basic ways of overcoming the problem: to generate electricity with the tidal flow and then store the electricity for later use, or to find a more sophisticated way of controlling the water flow through the turbines by, for example, storing the tidal water in more than one basin and pumping it around the system. The latter solution is more efficient but costs more to build, the former is cheaper but less satisfactory—a case here for exercising the British genius in the art of compromise.

The working party's general conclusion was that the scheme looked feasible and that there was a good case for going ahead with some more detailed research. At the time it seemed that it was not particularly attractive as an economic proposition, but they recognized that it was likely to become more acceptable as time passed and fuel costs rose. A similar conclusion was reached by a committee headed by the distinguished scientist Hermann Bondi. Both agreed that the most likely site for a barrage was between Sand Point near Weston-super-Mare and Lavernock Point, south of Cardiff. Technical problems are clearly going to be enormous, but at least civil engineers have gained valuable experience, first at the Rance site and then with the tidal barrage across the Thames. The latter was authorized not to provide power but to control the tides in order to prevent a possible, some might say probable, flooding of central London. The objective might be different but the engineering problems have many points of similarity, not the least of which is keeping the river navigable.

The Thames barrage is one of this century's most impressive engineering feats as far as Britain's rivers are concerned. The river itself has to be kept open for normal purposes, so some sort of gate had to be supplied. With the widest gap being 200 feet, no swinging gates would answer. The force needed to move such a structure through water would be vast. The answer had to be a gate that moved vertically. One obvious answer might seem to be a portcullis-type arrangement, but here again there is a snag. To lift such a gate clear of ships' masts, its towers would have had to be huge. So the designers decided to go down rather than up, with gates that lie on the river bed and can then be raised into place to form a flood barrier right across the river in a quarter of an hour. Once it is completed, London should at last be safe from floods.

With the barrage providing a more controlled flow of water in the river, a scheme such as that on the Severn could improve navigation. What is uncertain is the effect of such a huge artificial obstacle on the natural life of the river. It is one mark of changing attitudes in the second half of the twentieth century that such a question should be considered at all. The Victorians would have built first and asked such 'secondary' questions later, if at all. We are just beginning to appreciate how valuable our rivers are as natural assets.

The great scourge of rivers in the nineteenth century was pollution—from sewage, industrial waste and the general muck and filth of the towns. Few people bothered much at first, mainly because they were too busy with their own affairs to spare time for such matters as dirty rivers. It was the increase in leisure that did more than anything to make people aware of the problem. We are now beginning to realize that conservation is more than an electioneering catch phrase or a subject espoused by a variety of freaks, who have beards, wear sandals and only eat vegetables. It has finally become obvious that it is the conservationists who are making sense—the issue affects us all. As the urban environment becomes progressively more dreary with rows of enlarged boxes dominating the skyline, we are coming to appreciate the pleasure of 'getting away from it all'. It is a sad reflection on the best efforts of well-meaning planners, that the first reaction to their efforts is an overwhelming desire to get away from them as quickly as possible. Rivers offer a route away from drab conformity, but who wants to spend their time on the river bank watching yesterday's meals drift by on the current? People want their rivers to be clean, to be beautiful and to be a home to wild life. They are beginning to see their wishes come true.

One of the great success stories of recent years has been that of the reclamation of the tidal Thames. Thanks to a combination of strict anti-pollution laws and positive efforts to overcome problems like sewage disposal, the river has, quite literally, been revitalized. Industrialists along the river have cooperated in the great clean-up, and the local authorities, who in the past have been among the worst pollutants, have worked hard to put their own house in order. The results have been spectacular. A 1957 study revealed the Thames to be a completely dead river—nothing lived there, nothing could live there. Twenty years later, and there has been a revolution. No less than 3,000 fish were collected in one sample in the Dartford area, mostly whiting, though a number of other fresh- and salt-water fish, ranging from haddock to pike, were included. There is even talk—cautious talk only at the moment—that the noble salmon might yet again be seen in London's river.

Other rivers are undergoing similar improvements, which is good news for everyone. A living river has more than just fish to recommend it. Birds thrive on the clean waters, and especially those which, like the heron, take advantage of the improved fishing prospects. Seeing those still, grey birds suddenly snake out their long necks to spear a fish with unerring accuracy makes one realize that we poor humans are mere beginners in the fishing business. Plant and animal life thrive together, and while no one is suggesting that the Thames in London will ever be one of the great fishing rivers of Britain, it is a lovely thought that one day you might be able to get a salmon at somewhere other than Billingsgate Market. Given time, the Thames could be what the Seine is for Paris, a river for the city dweller to enjoy—a place to rest beside and watch the boats go by or to get out rod and line to attempt to reduce the fish population.

At various times the accolade 'most popular sport' is awarded to all kinds of different activities, but if one looks at the matter in terms of active participants instead of mere spectators, then fishing is never far from the top of the list. For some of us, of course, fishing is also a spectator sport. Whatever attributes are required to lure fish from the water, we lack them. We see others do it, with quite disgusting regularity, and we even see them throw back, with a disgruntled snort, specimens we would be pathetically proud to hook. But then, there is also a certain value in the fishing rod as an excuse for just sitting quietly by the water. The world of the dedicated angler allows no such luxuries. It is full of subtleties and nuances, which bewilder the outsider. And to read, as one did in March 1980, that a length of the Tay is to be sold for salmon fishing at the cost of hundreds of thousands of pounds leaves the outsider bewildered. The world of the coarse fisherman is at least more comprehensible in financial terms. The early morning pilgrimage to the river in pursuit of bream, chub or pike is made every weekend of the season by anglers in their tens of thousands. One of the great attractions of the sport lies in the fact that you never lose. Even if nothing takes the carefully prepared bait, there is still a gain. The river is always there to share its delights with the patient watcher.

Modern attitudes towards rivers are, in many ways, a simple continuation of attitudes first shown by the romantics of the nineteenth century. They are the views encapsulated in four lines by Gerard Manley Hopkins:

> What would the world be, once bereft
> Of wet and of wildness? Let them be left—
> Let them be left. O, wildness and wet;
> Long live the weeds and the wilderness yet.

Those lines are today uttered with a new urgency, for man has placed the wilderness at risk. The city becomes ever more impersonal, and nature seems in retreat. Every architect's drawing, at one time, showed the inevitable little square beneath the inevitable large office block. It was full of cheery people, sitting beneath the trees or wandering around, having idle conversations. The square—or piazza as it became in plannerese—sometimes had little tables shaded by umbrellas, where summer drinks were sipped. It was never winter. The reality has been with us long enough to make such drawings a joke in poor taste. The little squares are miniature wind tunnels, where the only humans can be seen scuttling through tearing at the old newspapers that the wind has wrapped against their legs. More than ever we need the wilderness and the wet, and we need to fight to protect it.

Everyone who has ever known and loved the country will have his personal memories of astonishing beauty: the sight of a heron playing statues by the water's edge, the electric flash of a kingfisher darting out over the water before disappearing back into the dark of the trees, the calm of early morning when the mist sits on the water. Often such glimpses have nothing to do with established beauty spots, but come from an accidental conjunction of circumstances. I remember such a morning beside Hebden Water in Yorkshire. The fog had smothered the land like a blanket since dawn, until at around mid-day the blanket began to tear apart. Through the rents, the mill chimneys appeared first, like triumphant columns. Gradually as the fog cleared and I walked away from the town through the woods that line the river bank, a pale sun broke through. The fog still hung in the branches, but now the water drops gleamed like tiny lanterns, and the water threw back the reflections. It was a magical transformation that lasted only for a few moments, but long enough to imprint the image on the memory. Equally, even a famous beauty spot can have its surprises. It is easy to forget that such spots actually are beautiful and not put there by some wily entrepreneur in the tourist industry. Out of season, the old magic can return. Bolton Abbey beside the Wharfe is justly popular, but in winter with snow on the ground, the dark walls of the ruin are thrown into relief and the river in full flow thunders through the narrow gulley known as the Strid, as exciting a sight as the most impressive waterfalls.

We need the beauty of our rivers and we need their wildness, yet all the time we are making other demands. We need more water for our homes and for industry. We need to grow more food, so we spread chemicals on the land which wash down into the water. We want growth but we have also reached the point where we must ask—growth to what end? Increased productivity will, we are told, increase wealth and leisure—but what if there is nothing worth while left for our leisure and nothing worth while on which to spend our wealth? The rivers must provide one important part of the answer, for it is still possible to conserve much of the river environment. Some years ago, the author and photographer, Eric de Maré, proposed creating a linear national park along the Upper Thames, preserving the immediate river environment. Why not, and why not extend the idea to other rivers? It is not impossible and the rewards could be immense. The need is growing for such retreats and already a way of using the rivers for leisure has been found in an adaptation of one of its major industrial uses of previous centuries.

The building of river navigations formed a prelude to the canal age. The navigation authorities feared the canals would take their trade, and prophesied doom. The canals actually increased river traffic. They feared the coming of railways, yet trade survived to a far greater extent than they prophesied. They said that the motor lorry would kill off most of their trade—this time they were right. What they did not prophesy was that a new trade would be born on the old navigations—pleasure boating. To the Victorians and Edwardians, a day on the river meant punt or skiff or, for the wealthy few, the steam launch. Today skiff and punt are more or less relegated to the hourly outing, an afternoon poling along, or falling into, some quiet backwater. The motor boat has increasingly taken over the navigable rivers. Throughout the summer months, the popular rivers are busy with a bewildering variety of holiday craft. The modern holiday cruiser can be metal or fibreglass, sleek or bulbous, a design based on traditional forms or a floating bath tub. Occupants of these vessels are equally varied: cheery families sharing the water with stern men who captain their craft as though they were bringing in a Cunarder. Some rivers are so crowded with boats that one feels saturation point cannot be far away. One solution to that problem has been to look for more rivers to travel. Old navigations that had fallen into disuse, whose locks had seemed no more than piles of rubble, have been and are being restored.

The first river navigation to be given this treatment was the Warwickshire Avon. In the 1940s, the Lower Avon from Evesham to the Severn at Tewkesbury was virtually unnavigable, and seemed destined to return to nature. The Midlands Inland Waterways Association, led by C. D. Barwell, had other ideas. They actually managed to raise enough money, £1,500, to buy the Navigation, at which point they formed the Lower Avon Navigation Trust, and then began to raise more money so that volunteers could begin the work of restoration. That was in 1950. Twelve years and £35,000 later, the navigation was re-opened. It was the forerunner of many such schemes.

In the same region, David Hutchings, a local architect, took charge of a motley array of workers—enthusiasts prepared to give up their spare time to work for nothing, volunteer prisoners who preferred the open air to mail bag stitching and soldiers looking for a chance to practice some basic engineering. They got together to work on the southern end of the Stratford Canal for the National Trust. That was completed in 1964, and now there was another tempting prospect for Hutchings. If the Upper Avon could also be restored, then boats could pass all the way from Birmingham via Stratford to the Severn and then come back via the Severn and the Worcester and Birmingham Canal to where they had started. He set to work as he had on the Stratford Canal and the Avon ring was closed. It has become one of the most popular cruising routes in the country. Other schemes have followed—the restoration, for example, of the Kennet Navigation and the Wey and Arun. The objective has been to supply cruising routes, but at the same time there has been a revival of interest in the history of these old navigations.

The history of navigable rivers is closely associated with the craft that used them. It is only recently that we have come to appreciate what a rich variety of boats there once was on Britain's rivers—and the realization came almost too late. Take the case of the Severn trow. Once there were hundreds on the river: today there are none. The last surviving vessel was the *Spry*, built in 1894 at one of the major shipyards that specialized in these craft, Hurd's of Chepstow. She spent her final days as a floating workshop, moored up at Diglis Basin, just off the Severn at the entrance to the Worcester and Birmingham Canal. She sank, but was raised in 1977 and the Severn Trow Preservation Society are restoring her to full working condition. They have good grounds for believing that they will succeed, for already there are a number of local societies who have managed to get similar old craft back under sail when all seemed lost. Norfolk wherry and Humber keel can again be seen on the water. And restoration itself can be a fascinating process. The sight of an old craft gradually being brought back to life gladdens the heart of any boat lover—and when one can see it in a truly beautiful setting, then what more could you want? One of the pleasantest of restorations was that of the Tamar sailing barge, *Shamrock*, at Calstock on the west bank of the river. The surroundings are perfect: the wharf with its old stone buildings and wharfers' cottages, while nearby are the big stone lime kilns which once provided a good part of the cargo. But if one had to pick on a single restoration scheme which had a particular and very special appeal then one might well turn to East Anglia.

The River Stour Trust was formed in 1968 with the aim of restoring navigation on the twenty-four-mile-long river made famous by the greatest of British landscape artists, John Constable. He himself wrote: 'I associate my "careless boyhood" to all that lies on the banks of the *Stour*.' He has left us memorable images of the river: Flatford Mill in many seasons and many lights, river locks, boat building and numerous paintings of Stour lighters. One of the tasks of the Trust has been to restore a lighter which was dug out of the mud in a sorry condition, but which will one day be a reality to set alongside the images in Constable's paintings. The Trust have also been hard at work restoring the old eighteenth-century navigation basin at Sudbury which is still dominated by the old granary, now the Quay Theatre. They have already restored Flatford lock and would do more, but they are faced by powerful opposition. It is a sad fact that most of the Trust's energies and enthusiasms, not to mention funds, have had to be deployed in facing those who simply do not wish to see boats back on the river. The chief opponents are the anglers and, to some extent, the boating community have only themselves to blame. On too many rivers you can see boats travelling far too fast, making a huge wash and disturbing the peace of other river users. Yet there must be very many people who belong to neither camp who would love to see the lighter out again on the waters of Constable's river.

Boating is an increasingly popular and, unfortunately, an increasingly noisy occupation, but the hardy can always leave the noise behind. One way to overcome the problem of lack of navigable rivers is to take to those rivers which are nominally unnavigable, but which can be travelled by the right sort of craft. The kayak canoe has opened up new rivers and provided new opportunities for enjoying river scenery. One of the most popular rivers for canoe touring is the Wye, much of which is perfect for the beginner with just a few simple rapids to give a sense of danger and excitement. The sense is not altogether illusory. Having managed to turn through 180° and shoot the rapids backwards (not from choice) and then sunk the canoe elsewhere, this is one amateur canoeist who found the Wye quite exciting enough. The rewards for perseverance, though, are immense. The Wye offers some justly famous scenery, reaching a dramatic climax as it sweeps in a great semicircle round the high promontory of Symonds Yat. Those who are both more competent and more adventurous can get all the excitement they want on the upper reaches of the Wye, while the true enthusiasts compete among the white waters of the Dee near Llangollen. Canoeing is not a pastime for the untrained, but those who take the trouble to learn the art under proper tuition find a whole new river world to explore.

Some have found pleasure in another form of exploration, following rivers underground. Caving is one of those pastimes one either loves or loathes; for some of us the first pot-hole was also the last. To the true enthusiast, however, it offers access to some of the last truly lonely and wild places in the country. On the surface, every river has been crossed and recrossed, explored, examined and mapped. Underground there is still a genuinely unknown world to explore, and puzzles to be answered. The underground courses of rivers can often be mysterious, as the river eats through the soft rock and wriggles round the hard. It is a world of admitted danger, but also one of beauty—a beauty which comes with all the freshness of surprise. Above ground, we know, in most cases, before we set out that a river valley will offer certain specific delights. We can sometimes be caught unawares when an accident of light and circumstance stops us in delighted amazement. Underground, there must be whole regions of literally unknown beauty, which no man has ever seen. That is just one of the lures that draw the caver back to the wet and the dark.

Our present age has seen a shift of emphasis. Rivers could again become an important source of energy, and we may find it necessary to reverse the trends of the past hundred years and expand rather than contract their use for transport. In a crowded world, we are going to look to them more and more as escape routes to a quieter way of life. But we face contradictions. Can we expand commercial use without endangering leisure use? Is there not a real possibility that the increased leisure use will be self-defeating, since there is a limit to the number of people who can seek peace and quiet in the same place? Is there not also a possibility that new developments will necessarily destroy the beauty of the rivers? The worst may yet happen, but there is no reason to suppose that it must happen. Twentieth-century engineers have shown that they can build structures of as much grace and with as much style as their predecessors. Take two examples of bridges built to a very different scale—the Severn Road Bridge and Ove Arup's Kingsgate Bridge at Durham. Any of the great engineers and architects of the past would have been proud to claim them. We know that we do not have to behave like mindless barbarians, spreading ugliness across the land. We are going to have to come to terms with such problems, for in the future world of energy shortages, the rivers look likely again to become 'veins in the national body'. We should do well to remember, however, that we do not own the rivers, we only share the land with them. T. S. Eliot expressed it perfectly in the *Four Quartets*:

> I do not know much about gods; but I think that the river
> Is a strong brown god—sullen, untamed and intractable,
> Patient to some degree, at first recognized as a frontier;

Useful, untrustworthy, as a conveyor of commerce;
Then only a problem confronting the builder of bridges.
The problem once solved, the brown god is almost forgotten
By the dwellers in cities—ever, however, implacable,
Keeping his seasons and rages, destroyer, reminder
Of what men choose to forget.

We may use the river, even claim rights over it, but in the end it belongs only to itself. The rivers of Britain have served us well in the past, and will no doubt serve us well in the future. We should respect them.

Bibliography

There are literally hundreds of books dealing with various aspects of rivers and river life; so many, that it would be impossible to list them all. The following is a list of books and papers quoted directly in the text, combined with those books which are particularly valuable as further reading on particular aspects of the subject.

Abstract of Rules, Orders and constitution of the Company of Watermen and Lightermen, 1708

Anon, *A River Holiday*, 1883

Anon, *A Tour in Teesdale*, 1804

Aston, Michael and Bond, James, *The Landscape of Towns*, 1976

Ayton, Richard, *A Voyage Round Great Britain*, 1814

Barnard, Alfred, *Noted Breweries of Great Britain and Ireland*, 1889

Barnard, Alfred, *The Whisky Distilleries of the United Kingdom*, 1887

Barton, N. J., *The Lost Rivers of London*, 1962

Berners, Juliana, *Treatyse of Fysshynge wyth an Angle*, 1496

Burton, Anthony, *Remains of a Revolution*, 1974

Burton, Anthony and Pip, *The Green Bag Travellers*, 1978

Carr, Frank G. C., *Sailing Barges*, 1951

Chartres, J. A., 'Road Carrying in England in the Seventeenth Century', *Economic History Review*, 1977

Collingwood, R. J., and Myres, J. N. L., *Roman Britain and the English Settlements*, 1937

A Commissioner, *Extracts from the Navigation Rolls of the River Thames and Isis*, 1772

de Maré, Eric, *Bridges of Britain*.

de Maré, Eric, *Time on the Thames*, 1952

de Salis, Henry, *Canals and Navigable Rivers of England and Wales*, 1904

Dixon Hunt, John and Willis, Peter, *The Genius of the Place, the English Landscape Garden*, 1975

Doxat, John, *The Living Thames*, 1977

Dyer, John, *The Fleece*, 1757

Edwards, Lewis A., *Inland Waterways of Great Britain and Ireland*, 1962

Ekvall, Eilert, *English River Names*, 1928

Engels, Frederick, *The Condition of the Working Class in England in 1844*, 1892

Farr, Graham E., *Chepstow Ships*, 1954

The Fisher's Garland, 1821–32

Fletcher, Henry, *A Life on the Humber*, 1975

'A genuine Dicky Sam', *Liverpool and Slavery*, 1884

Gilpin, William, *Observations on the River Wye*, 1770

Hadfield, Charles, *British Canals*, 1974

Hawksmoor, Nicholas, *A Short Historical Account of London Bridge*, 1736

Hinton, David A., *Alfred's Kingdom*, 1977

Hornell, James, *Water Transport—Origins and Early Evolution*, 1946

Jerome, Jerome K., *Three Men in a Boat*, 1889

Jervoise, E., *The Ancient Bridges of the South of England*, 1930

Jervoise, E., *The Ancient Bridges of the North of England*, 1931

Mann, J. de L., *The Cloth Industry in the West of England*, 1971

Markham, Gervase, *The Young Sportsman's Instructor*, 1597

Mathew, Francis, *A Mediterranean Passage from London to Bristol*, 1670

Mathew, Francis, *A Mediterranean Passage between Lynn and Yarmouth*, 1656

Priestley, Joseph, *Navigable Rivers and Canals*, 1831

Reynolds, John, *Windmills and Watermills*, 1970

Robertson, H. R., *Life on the Upper Thames*, 1875

Rolt, L. T. C., *Isambard Kingdom Brunel*, 1957

Rolt, L. T. C., *Victorian Engineering*, 1970

Snell, Lawrence S., *Essays towards a History of Bewdley*, 1972

Stow, John, *A Survey of London*, 1598

Taylor, John, *An Arrant Thief*, 1622

Taylor, John, *The Description of the Famous Rivers of Thames and Isis*, 1632

Trueman, A. E., *Geology and Scenery in England and Wales*, 1949

Walton, Izaak, *The Compleat Angler*, 1653

Willan, T. S., *River Navigation in England, 1600–1750*, 1936

Woolridge, John, *The Art of Gardening*, 1677

Yarranton, Andrew, *England's Improvement by Sea and Land*, 1677

Index